BEHOLD, HE COMES

Meditations on the Incarnation

Fr. Benedict Groeschel, C.F.R.

CHARIS

SERVANT PUBLICATIONS
ANN ARBOR, MICHIGAN

Charis Books is an imprint of Servant Publications especially designed to serve Roman Catholics.

Published by Servant Publications
P.O. Box 8617
Ann Arbor, Michigan 48107

Cover design by Alan Furst, Inc. - Minneapolis, MN

01 02 03 10 9 8 7 6 5 4 3 2 1

Printed in the United States of America
ISBN 0-56955-315-7

Library of Congress Cataloging-in-Publication Data
Groeschel, Benedict J.
    Behold, He Comes : meditations on the incarnation / Benedict Groeschel.
        p. cm.
    Includes bibliographical references.
    ISBN 1-56955-315-7 (alk. paper)
    1. Incarnation—Meditations. I. Title.
    BT220 .G82 2001
    242' .33—dc21

                                                                2001002920

BEHOLD, HE COMES

Meditations on the Incarnation

INTRODUCTION

This series of meditations, although prepared for the specific days of Advent and the Christmas season, can also be used as meditations on the Incarnation, the mystery of the eternal Word of God taking to himself a human body and a human soul.

The coming of the Son of Man into this world is the most important event that ever did or ever could happen. Every year the Church celebrates this event at Christmas, although the Gospels do not tell us the date of Christ's birth. Very early on, the Church linked the birth of Christ with a winter holiday observed in the ancient Roman Empire. By observing Christmas toward the end of December, the Church hoped to Christianize a pagan celebration that marked the "birth of the sun," or the first days following winter solstice, when the sun began to remain for a few minutes more each day in the sky.

I have tried to make these readings fully appropriate for Christians of all traditions, not just Catholics. The meditations are not scriptural commentaries or even thoughts on the liturgy of the day. Rather they are meant to focus the reader's mind and heart on the Scriptures and the traditional interpretation of these Scriptures.

From the fourth to the eighth centuries, the early Church and its shepherds were deeply concerned about preserving and defending the biblical accounts of the Incarnation of the Word of God. These early bishops and theologians focused on the whole of revelation, and they worked out a series of teachings, or dogmas, which have guided believers through the centuries. The principal Protestant reformers never disputed these teachings; as a result, they form the Christology (or belief about Christ) of almost all devout Christians throughout the world.

Unfortunately, in recent decades a real ignorance of these teachings has developed, following a decline in religious education and interest in Church history. I have been very careful to present these ancient teachings in an authentic and compelling way. Sadly, even in classrooms and in the pulpit one can hear erroneous and false teachings, indicating inadequate theological knowledge of the Christology of the ancient Church. It is most disturbing to hear irresponsible positions, which are pure guesswork, put forward as facts or at least valid interpretations of New Testament texts. Moreover, these guesses are made without regard for the teachings of the early Christians who lived in the times and in the world where Christianity began.

I hope that you will find these short meditations helpful in two ways—to assist you to dwell on the mysteries of the Messiah, and also to prepare you to read the Gospels more deeply in the light of the original Christian interpretations. These interpretations were often done by men who faced martyrdom and total rejection. Many died for their faith in Christ. Later the teachings of the early Church were focused on controversies when false teachings like Arianism spread through the ancient world.

How to Use This Book

These ideas for meditation can be used quite apart from the Christmas season. Occasionally the celebration of saints' days—some ancient like John and Stephen, some modern like John Neumann and Brother André—will be included. I have attempted to link these celebrations with the general theme of Christmas.

The book has been divided into two parts. Part One contains a series of daily reflections for the seasons of Advent and Christmas, which are related to the Gospel reading assigned to the day's liturgy. Part Two contains additional prayers, hymns, and other spiritual readings on the Incarnation that may be read throughout the year. However, these too are especially appropriate reading as we prepare to celebrate the Savior's birth.

Before you begin to read each day's meditation, I suggest that you first begin with an earnest prayer to the Holy Spirit to guide you. Next take a period of silence to reflect that you are in the presence of Jesus Christ, who dwells in the soul of every Christian who is united with Him by divine grace.

If you are a Catholic and can make these meditations before the Holy Eucharist where Christ is present in his Body and Blood, all the better. While you are there, you may also wish to reflect upon the hymns and prayers in the second part of this book, or from another source such as the liturgically centered thoughts and meditations of *Magnificat*.[1] Spending time with the Lord in this manner is beneficial to your spiritual growth.

Read the meditation thoughtfully and prayerfully. Let it sink in, so to speak. The short oration at the end of the meditation is to help you formulate your own prayer. This may be quite different from my oration. Your own prayer will help you to have a thought for the day emerging from the impact of grace on your own inner life. This in turn will help you each day to be a better follower of Christ.

As always, I am very indebted to my friend and associate Charles Pendergast for his assistance in publishing this book. He prepared the entire manuscript and did much research, as he has done for so many of my books. I also want to thank Bert Ghezzi and all at Servant Publications for encouraging me to do this work. I hope to share it with many who have assisted our Franciscan community in our work with the poor. I also hope to follow it up with other meditations on the life of Christ.

—Father Benedict J. Groeschel, C.F.R

St. Crispin Friary

Bronx, New York

Feast of the Annunciation 2001

Part One

DAILY MEDITATIONS

From the First Day of Advent
Through the Baptism of the Lord

ADVENT—WEEK 1
The First Sunday

"The light shines in the darkness, and the darkness has not overcome it" (John 1:5).

Advent calls us as Christians to ponder again the mystery of our salvation, our hope that there is an answer to the riddle of earthy life with its passing joys, disappointments, sorrows, and frustrations, and its apparently dark end in the oblivion of death.

Does life go anywhere? Does it have any meaning? Advent calls every one of us to stop in the struggle of life and to look up, to recall the answer to the questions of life. We are on a journey to our Father's house. The door has been opened to us by the Son of God, and the way marked out.

Advent invites us to look back over the long centuries, during which the human race struggled on in shadows. Of course, there was always some light. It began with the promise of a Redeemer who would crush the head of the destroying Serpent, the Son of a woman at bitter enmity with evil.

The experience of human beings during those thousands of years of waiting is not so different from the lives of those around us who live without the consolation of faith and hope. They can accomplish much, but to what purpose? They can struggle to live as well and as long as possible, but then they will sorrow as those who have no hope.

The Christian should look at and listen to this darkness and confusion. Human existence for the believer is always an advent, a waiting, a journey toward a destination, toward the light. Begin Advent by recalling the long darkness endured by the human race. Many are still in it.

As believers, we have the faith to know that God came to us through no merit of our own, and that He comes to us still by His grace. He calls to us by His birth, His life, His terrible death, and His glorious Resurrection. Advent reminds us that He will come again.

So many mysteries, so many questions, and so many answers. For the one with faith, Advent should be a time of mystery, discovery, new insights, and deeper joy.

Prayer

God of life and eternity, God of mystery, You called our lost race out of darkness long ago, promising to send the One who would deliver us from evil and death. The darkness of life remains, but it does not prevail. Give me Your Holy Spirit, so that I may stop and think and pray as I live again through the long time of expectation and prepare to celebrate that our Redeemer has come. Help me to learn from the events of His life how much You love your children, and will that they return to You. Amen.

ADVENT—WEEK 1
Monday

"I am the light of the world" (*John 8:12*).

We all have times when life seems meaningless, especially when we lose those we love through estrangement or death. Often we put much effort and even love into something we value, only to have it taken away. But we go on with the belief that all of this struggle means something, that our lives have some purpose, that existence is not a black hole.

For the believing Christian, this experience of meaninglessness is simply the opportunity for faith and hope. Discouragement, even desperation, can make our act of faith in Christ's saving grace all the more real. We are following our Savior on His journey to His Father's house, but because we live in an unbelieving world, we can be drawn into the hopelessness of unbelief without ever noticing it.

By accident I once saw part of a James Bond movie—a world of clever and vicious animals, like creatures with human faces but without hearts or souls. This is what the world would have been like without the grace of God and the promise of salvation. Advent must remind us of that possibility. I could cry when I think of all the decent people who live without hope. Christians must pray for these people, that they would experience Advent—literally the time of His coming—in their own lives. At the same time, we must be ever more grateful that we know that the Light has come, and is here with us even now.

Prayer

Jesus, my Lord, You have come into our dark world with the promise of eternal life, giving our struggles meaning—beautiful and profound meaning. But help me to remember this supreme truth in the rough-and-tumble of daily life. Help me to live what I believe: You are the Way, the Truth, and the Life. By doing this consistently, may I show hope to those who have no hope. Amen.

ADVENT—WEEK 1
Tuesday

Down From the Stars

It is easy to become a practical materialist, to act as if everything can be weighed and measured, bought and sold. I can fall into the pattern of thinking that time, with its sixty minutes and twenty-four hours, is the real measure of my existence, and that what I possess makes me who I am. The coming of the Son of God into this material world shatters all of this. His coming puts all material things into true perspective.

There is an old Italian peasant hymn, written by Saint Alphonsus Liguori: "Tu scendi dalle stelle, O Re del cielo" ("You have come down from the stars, O King of heaven"). Although Saint Francis lived long before the hymn was written, one can imagine him singing these words at the first Christmas crib.

Christ comes from beyond the stars, beyond all material existence, beyond time and place and every change. He comes from what we call eternity, scarcely aware of what this word means when we say it. Yet we all have known that we shall face eternity when our life is over. And we catch glimpses of this mystery when someone dear to us dies. Did that person—my mother or father, my wife or husband, my child, my dear friend—did they go beyond the stars? Do they still exist? Will we meet them again? Advent opens for us the way beyond the stars, beyond the mystery of the material world, to the more unfathomable mystery of God's eternal life.

Prayer

O Lord Jesus Christ, You came from beyond the stars to live and die here and to rise and ascend to where You had come from. And You call us: "Follow me." Lord, we are creatures of clay. That's what human nature means—from the humus, the soil. Without Your helping hand we cannot follow You. But You continue to call us by the example of Your holy life, by Your incredible death and startling Resurrection. Increase my faith so that I may more and more believe that You have come from the Father and that You return to Him, calling us to follow. Amen.

ADVENT—WEEK 1
Wednesday

"Fall on Your Knees"

Like so many precious things, Advent can be, and often is, trivialized. Advertisers and merchants use every type of media to sell things for the winter holidays. And while giving gifts is not a bad thing, it can become simply a duty, a custom, even a resented burden.

At the same time, behind all the tinsel and triviality of the season, there is something very important. Our Lord Jesus Christ calls it the "mystery of the kingdom of God." And it has been given to us to believe and to know this mystery. The coming of our Lord is a mystery.

Not long ago I heard of a seminary teacher referring to the coming of the Lord as a myth. Christ's Incarnation, in which He takes on Himself a human body and soul, is not a myth. How silly and even deceptive it is to use such a term referring to the mysteries of God. Myths are made by human beings. They can be used to communicate some truth, like George Washington and his cherry tree. But a myth is an idea or image you can interpret any way you like. Santa Claus is a myth. He can be the historical figure Saint Nicholas of Myra, bishop of Bari, from whom the Santa Claus image is drawn. Or he can be the silly old elf holding a gigantic bottle of whiskey in the liquor store window.

Jesus Christ is not a myth. He is the mystery of God. Einstein described a mystery as a reality we can perceive but not penetrate with our human mind—a reality filled with wonder and beauty. This great scientist called the appreciation of mystery the cradle of all science and art and the truest expression of religious experience.

Advent calls the thoughtful soul to ponder the mystery of Christ the Lord. This mystery should put us prayerfully on our knees. "Who shall stand when He appears?" the prophet asks. The answer is, only a fool stands when He appears. A wise person falls and kneels at least in mind and heart.

Prayer

Lord Jesus Christ, You came and we did not fall on our knees. We stand, we stroll, we skip, and try to enjoy the tinsel. Give us Your Holy Spirit that we may fall on our knees, entranced by the mystery. The Scriptures and the prayer of the Church call us in Advent to fall on our knees and to the angel voices. Give us, O blessed Child of God, the grace to fall on our knees and to listen in adoration. Amen.

ADVENT—WEEK 1
Thursday

"Blessed is he who comes in the name of the Lord"
(Psalm 118:26).

Who is it that comes? Any well-trained child can tell you simply, "Jesus is coming." That statement suffices for children, but its simplicity contains so many truths. The friars of our community have a custom of welcoming the great crowds who come to the Christmas crib in St. Patrick's Cathedral. Children and many adults want to touch or even reverently kiss the smiling statue of the Infant Christ. Behind this simple gesture are so many mysteries of the kingdom of God. In these meditations we will try during the days of Advent to prayerfully explore the question, Who is this? Who is He that comes in the name of the Lord? What does He bring with Him?

The smiling statue of the holy Infant must be seen with the accompanying words: "I am the way, the truth, and the life" (Jn 14:6) and "He who follows me will not walk in darkness" (Jn 8:12). What does it mean when He calls himself the way? Christ comes to teach us the road to salvation, the road beyond the end of our physical life, the road through the doors of death and beyond the grave to the other side, which He calls His kingdom.

How very important it is to receive Him as the way, the One who leads us to the reality that goes beyond all that we can think or imagine. He tells us that the way to eternal life is straight, the door narrow and hard to find. May He be merciful at the end as He has been during our lives. He not only comes but He also goes along the way that leads to life. And we must follow Him, or all is in vain.

Prayer

Lord Jesus Christ, You who are the way, give us the grace to want to follow You and then to follow You carefully. This is no time to make exceptions, much less excuses. You left us the Scriptures and the Church to show us the way. Prevent us from looking back or strolling around. We will find peace only if we follow You. Help us to struggle along the way, even to run on the way, for the life You promise lies ahead. Amen.

ADVENT—WEEK 1
Friday

"I am the way ..." (John 14:6).

The first thing noticed by anyone reading the Gospels carefully and prayerfully is that Jesus never compromises. He understands human nature. He is most compassionate to sinners who are repentant or, like the woman taken in adultery, simply endangered by their sin. He dines with those whom the world calls outcasts. But He never swerves, He never compromises, as we do. He comes to do the will of the Father, and He does it.

His well-known impatience with many human prescriptions and customs leaves a false impression that He was morally undemanding. And yet, as a devout Jew He was observant of the law, which in some real sense He had come to replace, or better to go beyond. He clearly said that the smallest jot of the law would remain. We live in an age that loves compromise, especially moral compromise, for the sake of convenience or pleasure. Our generation blithely dispenses itself even from one of the strictest and most obvious commandments—the commandment not to kill.

Christ never backed away from identifying sin where He saw it. His own moral teaching uncompromisingly demanded inner obedience and not just mere external observance of the divine law. He explicitly required inner chastity, fervent prayer, profound humility, forgiveness, and love. He required the loving care of the poor as a necessity of salvation. He never compromised the will of the Father. He could not, because He and the Father are one. To know Him is to know the living God and holiness itself.

Prayer

O Lord, show us again the way. Over and over again remind us that we do not mark out the way for ourselves, deciding what we would like the way to be, and altering it as we travel along it. You tell us that such a procedure is perilous. You alone are always our way. You are always our shepherd and call us on in the right way that leads to life. Amen.

ADVENT—WEEK 1
Saturday

"His heart was moved with pity ... they were like sheep without a shepherd" (Matthew 9:37).

In the midst of all the challenging thoughts that Advent may bring, we need to recall that Jesus Christ also came bringing the pity and compassion of God. Why did this divine Person come as a human being to endure pain, suffering, fatigue, and death—experiences He could never have had as God? The mysterious answer echoes through the whole New Testament: "God so loved the world that he gave his only Son, that whoever believes in him should ... have eternal life" (Jn 3:16).

Christ did not come to establish a Christian culture, although one gradually formed around His teaching and His Church. He did not come to heal all the sick or to raise all the dead. He did not come to win glory for Himself or even for His Father, because whatever glory we could give Him would be very insignificant indeed when compared with His own eternal glory as God. The fact is that He came out of compassionate love to save a fallen, doomed world. Without his coming, the only greatness of our race would have been the magnitude of its catastrophe. Hidden in the mist of the past, in the simple but startling account of man's Fall is an evil so awesome, so large in its scope of misery, so filled with hopelessness and suffering that we can hardly imagine it.

The human race, although struggling along in darkness, has never existed without hope and the unseen grace of redemption. The mercy

23

of God, through the promise of the Savior, reached out to every human being. Among all peoples were many who despite the darkness led good lives by reason of the grace of the promise. All human beings before Him unknowingly awaited His arrival, His Advent. He comes with all the power of God's love for the world. He comes because of his mercy, to show mercy to us.

Prayer

Lord Jesus, give me an increase of Your Holy Spirit that I may appreciate the gift of Your coming. Because of You there is light in every darkness and hope in the worst of human situations. The humility of Your birth may cause us not to see its eternal greatness. Help us to realize that the Lord has come with mercy and healing. Amen.

ADVENT—WEEK 2
The Second Sunday

"I am ... the truth" (John 14:6).

The smiling figure of the Infant of Bethlehem is a consolation to many people. What could be less threatening than a little baby?

And yet, that Bambino Gesù is the Son of God. When we see a newborn infant, the person has existed for only nine months. He or she has had little chance to function. The personality—the means by which the person interacts with the rest of the world—has hardly developed at all. Already there are the first cries, the first confrontation with reality. Soon there will be first smiles. A new person is beginning who will exist forever. For this reason every child conceived and born is a mystery.

But the Child of Bethlehem is not a new person. He always existed. He did not *become* God; He has always been God. Do not be deceived by His physical dependency. His body, like those of all new infants, must be held and supported. But His Person comes from beyond time and space and all limitations. His mother's heart is filled with the joy of all good mothers, but she also adores. As a devout Jew, she knew what it meant when the celestial messenger said to her, "He ... will be called the Son of the Most High; and the Lord God will give to Him the throne of His father David ... and of His kingdom there will be no end" (Lk 1:32–33).

Here is the first test of faith for the believer. Here is the mystery of God, and men dismiss it now as once they found no room for Him in the inns of Bethlehem. His coming is so shrouded in mystery, His being so incomprehensible: the human and divine, so incompatible, are now united. But we want to take the easy way out. It is a myth, a fairy tale.

This Child will grow to be a man. He will speak the truth as no one has ever spoken it. "I have come into the world to bear witness to the truth" (Jn 18:37). Truth must always be received with joy, awe, and gratitude. This is how we must receive this Child and learn from Him, because He will say, "Everyone who is of the truth hears My voice" (Jn 18:37).

Prayer

Jesus, my Savior, teach me the truth. Speak to me in the depths of my heart that I may return prayerfully in my thoughts to the humility of the manger. Let Your grace drive away my fear of a humble God with the body of an infant and the soul of a human child linked to the Person of God. Be the truth for me. Let me bow my stiff neck before the living Truth, which is so far beyond my limited mind. Amen.

ADVENT—WEEK 2
Monday

"Behold, your God will come. . . . The eyes of the blind shall be opened, and the ears of the deaf unstopped" (Isaiah 35:4-5).

Any serious person looking back thoughtfully on a few decades of life will realize that even with the best of teachers and guides we have been blind to many truths, or at least to their meaning. This is why we read the Scriptures and especially the Gospels over and over again. As our eyes open to the truth, we learn more and more each time we read them.

Sometimes books of the saints can do the same thing. For fifty years I have been reading Saint Augustine's *Confessions* and sermons, as well as the life of Saint Francis, and they are always new to me. This is because the eyes of the mind and the ears of the heart are being opened and cleared in the process of growing in the grace of Christ. His light and word never change, but we change and grow in our ability to see and hear Him.

This is why the Christian life, when properly understood, can never be boring. Boredom is a clear symptom that we are not growing, that we have lost the meaning of these words: "Behold, I make all things new" (Rv 21:5). The reasons for our blindness, deafness, and boredom are not difficult to discern. We are entranced by the sight of what is vain and passing, and captured by sounds that mean little or nothing.

Even in the most passing things we can find God's words, but only if we look and listen. Our desires and our hearts are impure: we want God, but we want many other things besides. It could be so easy to escape this emptiness, to find God in all that we see, hear, and experience. *The Imitation of Christ* tells us that if our hearts are pure, every creature will be for us a mirror of God and a book of holy teaching.

Why, then, don't we change? Because we cannot change, we cannot escape our blindness and deafness until we are healed by Jesus Christ. "Lord, that I may see," said the blind beggar of Jericho. Advent is a time to begin again, to appreciate, to value above all other things the coming of Him who is the light of the world for blind eyes and the Word of God for deaf ears. Come, Lord Jesus!

Prayer

O Christ Jesus, You and You alone are our truth. You help us to know things as they are. Help us to measure all our plans, all our values, all our desires by Your words and truth alone. If we are called to teach someone, may we teach them only Your truth. If we learn from someone, may we learn only the truth which You taught and proclaimed. In this world noisy with its false ideas, with its long lies and silly questions, open our ears to You, the Truth, which never changes. Amen.

ADVENT—WEEK 2
Tuesday

"Lord, that I may see" (Mark 10:51).

The mysterious Child of Bethlehem would one day call Himself the light of the world and promise that those who follow Him would not walk in darkness. Many times in Scripture He is referred to as the light. A light is of no use to us unless we walk by it or see things in it. An unbelieving time, even if it "values" religion and treats believers with some respect, is without the light of life. No one can live and function effectively unless there is true light.

Some kinds of light are not true light. False lights, like a bonfire seen in the desert at night, have caused souls to perish, guided by a light that led them miles away from the safe trail. This is not true light. Similarly, dim light blends color and shadow in a way that reveals some things but obscures others. This is not true light, either. There is also dangerous light, like the sunlight that in excess can cause illness and even death.

Jesus is the true light, unlike any earthly light. His divine nature brings with it the promise of the light of endless day. Perhaps you have sometimes followed false lights or seen the reality of life only in the confusion of light and shadows. It is not unusual for experienced people who started on the road of life with enthusiasm to realize that they have followed false lights, or dim and confusing lights.

Advent is a time of enlightenment. The glitz of the worldly holiday is so painful to the eyes of the soul that we close our bodily eyes and try to find a light within. The divine light of Jesus Christ—the light that the darkness cannot overcome—is shining, however obscurely, in every soul enlightened by grace.

Those who live completely unaware of the divine light within them ought to examine their lives carefully to see whether they are indeed growing in the grace of God at all. Once the light of Christ begins to guide our steps, to shape our thoughts and words, to shine on every blessing we have received, then we will walk in the light like children of the light.

Prayer

Light of the world, Light of life, shine on me and those dear to me and on all the world. Open our dull eyes and focus our vision on Your presence all around us. Help us to see those we love, those we know, those in need, in the light of Your love for us all. Draw our vision away from vain and passing things, and help us to see Your presence ever more clearly and to rejoice in Your light. Amen.

ADVENT—WEEK 2
Wednesday

"And a little child shall lead them"
(Isaiah 11:6).

Children are fascinated by the figure of the Divine Child. They look at the Christmas crib and wonder: What child is this? Why is He so important? Even children growing up in families deprived of faith or religious observance wonder about the Christ Child. Why do so many people celebrate his birth?

In a useless attempt to relate to those without faith and to make the Scriptures less challenging to modern people, some Christians try to minimize the mystery of Christ. They can even pretend to tell you what the Christ Child knew or did not know. However, this Child did not come into being in His mother's womb like all other children. He always existed in the mysterious infinity of the Trinity. He comes to lead us. He began to lead us from the moment of his mysterious conception. And He leads the people of God forever. His reign shall have no end.

Let this thought, that Christ is God, startle you. Admit any difficulty to yourself. And then meditate on the Word of God, and observe those who knew Him well or who, like Saint Paul, encountered Him after His resurrection from the dead. Read what the saints have said about Him for twenty centuries. He leads us! We do not lead Him. He who alone knows the Father, teaches us.

We do not know more about Him than is necessary for us to know. Can a mortal man know God? Can the little mind of an infant contain knowledge of the eternal, the infinite? How can He lead us unless He knows? Divine knowledge does not break into His human consciousness. It's quite the reverse. He began to know things in a human way; He always knows them in a divine way that is utterly mysterious to us.

As we think of His coming, we must make a decision. Either we accept His mysterious being and fall on our knees in adoration or we decide that we are going to figure all this out. Either He leads us or we stand around being puzzled by Him. What do you think is your proper response and attitude? You need to decide this, because He comes.

Prayer

Lord Jesus Christ, You promised to send us your Spirit, the Holy Spirit. Send Him in abundance that He may teach us to pray, as we ought to pray, in adoration. Help us whenever doubts come, doubts that arise from the foolish belief that our minds can measure eternity and the things of God. Give us Your Holy Spirit that He may be our interior teacher. And increase our faith. Amen.

ADVENT—WEEK 2
Thursday

"When you see this, your heart will rejoice"
(Isaiah 66:14).

If you ask most people what December is about, they are likely to say, "Getting ready for Christmas." But go one step further and ask what *this* means. They will mention buying presents, preparing for guests, or visiting family for the holidays. If you say, "What about celebrating the mystery of the birth of the Son of God?" they will eye you suspiciously and with a tinge of embarrassment say, "Of course. That too." It was not always this way.

Older people can remember when there was real excitement. As children, we fasted from candy and made little sacrifices for the Christ Child. We saved what little we had to buy presents but also to give something to the poor or to the Church. And we were excited. We all knew of course that Christ was born long ago, but somehow this remembrance made it seem that He was coming again to us.

I recall serving Midnight Mass at the Dominican Sisters' mother-house and, looking up on Christmas Eve on the way to the chapel, there was a large bright star. I do not now know whether it was the planet Jupiter or Venus in the clear, cold sky. I literally jumped when I saw it. Jesus was coming to our town.

Some call this the magic of Christmas. It's not magic, of course. Magic is a trick—the appearance of something that actually is not there. Christmas is a mystery: that which is intangible, unseen, is really there. Christ is with us every day whenever we decide to turn to Him.

Prayer

Lord Jesus, increase our faith. Draw our eyes away from unimportant things and our hearts from what is shallow. Help us to feel the joy of the shepherds or the Magi. Give us a taste of the wonder of Mary and Joseph. Help us to share with those we love and all those we know the truly good news: The Lord comes. Amen.

ADVENT—WEEK 2
Friday

*"Say to those who are of a fearful heart,
'Be strong, fear not!'" (Isaiah 35:3).*

We who are believers in our secularized society often feel intimidated. We feel odd, out of line, and we often keep our beliefs to ourselves. We hold on in the midst of scandals and media attacks. We are not blown away when the TV or the papers celebrate some failure of a religious person. Understandably, we do tend to keep our heads down.

I recall with regret and embarrassment once being asked out of the blue to explain the real meaning of Christmas to a committee largely made up of people who did not believe in Christ at all. I stammered and stuttered and said really stupid things, hoping that they would accept something.

I should have simply said, "I believe that the Son of God was born into this world in a mysterious and marvelous way in order to save us." They might have been stunned, but they would not have been bored. I could not make these people believe; it was not my responsibility to do so. Our Savior said very clearly, "No one can come to me unless the Father who sent me draws him" (Jn 6:44).

It is not my task to give someone faith, but it is my responsibility to be a witness to Christ and, to use His words, to confess Him before men. Obviously this has to be done with charity, insight, dignity, and even, if possible, tact. A bit of humor may help too. But those who are searching for belief are not looking to be convinced. They are waiting to see whether those who say they believe allow their faith to direct their lives. They are not looking for an argument; they are waiting for believers to act like they believe. Obviously when it comes to living our faith in Jesus Christ, we must act like believers, and we must let others know that we believe indeed that God has come.

Prayer

Lord, give me courage. Let me not be frightened, intimidated, or silent. With a smile and joy help me to share the Good News, or at least let me look as though I really believe it. Let me not be fainthearted, but rather full-hearted and filled with wonder, generosity, and gratitude. Amen.

ADVENT—WEEK 2
Saturday

"John ... came to testify as a witness to the light"
(John 1:6).

Light and darkness, as we have seen, are frequent Advent themes. In East and West, when human beings have drawn closer to the God who made them, they spoke of light or of being enlightened. Some remarkable people said that they had experienced a divine light. But now the Light itself comes. Not a glow or a reflection or even an enlightenment, but the Light itself comes.

We all look for light but only when we are aware of the darkness. There are many darknesses. We experience confusion, ignorance, discouragement, rejection, and even dark storms within our own souls. The worst darkness is the one we do not even recognize. We think we are seeing, but actually we are stumbling on in the dark, often into a deeper darkness. Some give up hope and sink into a hopeless darkness. Worse yet, some embrace the darkness and tell themselves it is the light. Our Lord exclaims, "How great has their darkness become!" (see Mt 6:23).

John the Baptist, that startling Advent figure, is witness to the Light. He will point to Jesus and exclaim, "Behold the Lamb of God who takes away the sins of the world!" (Jn 1:29). We shy away from John. He is too strong, too uncompromising, too demanding, in a word, too much. But he is the messenger who prepares the way.

We sometimes ask ourselves, have we really accepted Jesus and His message? We might begin by asking, have we listened to John? Have we heard his words: "Prepare the way of the Lord, make his paths straight" (Mk 1:3)? How will we ever come to accept the light of Jesus if we turn away from John? We might read in the Gospel about this mysterious man and how Jesus loved him and even honored him by calling him a blazing light. Do we take John's advice and prepare the way of the Lord?

Prayer

Lord Jesus, how often I water down Your message, allowing myself to be compromised. How often I bargain with Your Word and ignore your counsel. Help me to make straight the way for You to come by an ever more honest faith, hope, and love. And let me start today. Amen.

ADVENT—WEEK 3
The Third Sunday

"Rejoice.... The Lord is near"
(Philippians 4:4-5).

Anyone can be happy, given the right set of circumstances; only the believer can rejoice. To rejoice is to have a joy that the world cannot take away. Such joy cannot be derived from a moment of sin or shallow success; it is much deeper, and cannot be taken away by time or chance or mishap or by the certainty of death.

There are other kinds of joy, of course. Respectable joy, such as what you see in old photographs of a party, or of a prize won at sports, or at a wedding reception. The joy of a new job, a new house, a new baby. Thank God for such joys. But they fade.

There is one joy that never fades. It is the joy of Christian hope. Sorrow cannot erode it, and time cannot carry it away. It is the joy of eternal life. While we may find ways to preserve some of the simple joys of life, true eternal joy outshines them all. For it is only in the humble birth of the Son of God that passing joys have some hope of not disappearing like shadows.

The Son of God was also a child of earth. His mother cuddled Him. The awe of the shepherds did not entirely displace ordinary feelings of delight at the sweet but mysterious baby. The people of His village were later surprised by His words and wisdom. He became one of us.

Rejoice because the passing joys of human life do not have to disappear forever. This Child will show us how to see them all in the mystery of endless day. Most precious of all joys are those that come from love. More than all else we do not want to be separated forever from those we love. He came that we may be forever with Him—and with them. Rejoice!

Prayer

Lord Jesus Christ, You reign in the joy of eternal life, in the complete fullness of life without end. But in Advent You invite us to think of You as a newborn child, as an infant, and as a little boy. Help us to know in this passing world that You can show us how to cherish forever the joys of this life so that they may not perish but be drawn into the joy of life without end. Amen.

ADVENT—WEEK 3
Monday

*"Make me to know thy ways, O Lord;
teach me thy paths" (Psalm 25:4).*

We all like to do our own thing, to follow our impulses or poorly thought-out convictions. A little life experience and a few moments of reflection on years gone by will usually cause an intelligent person to be aware of many mistakes in the past. Sometimes from the vantage point of present experience we wonder: "How could I ever have been so dumb?" It's only a small consolation to realize that the rest of the human race is in the same situation, only many don't seem to even realize it.

When it comes to the really important decisions of life, the believing Christian has a way out. God is our teacher. The Holy Spirit is our guide. Such sentiments at least start us in the right direction. However, it's just a start. The apostles, who knew Jesus as well as anyone but His own family, often failed to understand Him, and in the end they failed Him completely.

If we take the Gospel seriously, we see that most of His family, except His mother and her sister, the wife of Clopas, did not understand Him at all. Some even thought He was mad (see Mk 3: 21–22).

Sooner or later, most people who take Christ seriously wake up to the fact that we are not really following Him. We are trying to get Him to walk alongside us so that we can get support as we make our own decisions. We admit that His will is indeed happening all around us while we make other plans.

When Christ comes to us in our inner being, He reminds us: "I am the way, and the truth, and the life" (Jn 14:6). And again, "He who follows me will not walk in darkness" (Jn 8:12). Advent is a perfect time to remind ourselves that Jesus is the only true light. How much are we following Him? And how can we follow His teaching and example more closely?

Prayer

Lord Jesus, when You came, few understood You, and even Your followers often chose their own way. I want to be Your disciple, but I so often choose my own way. It is one thing for me to avoid sin, but it is quite another to follow You faithfully and completely. Help me today to follow You more closely and tomorrow even a bit more closely. Be a light to my steps and the teacher of my soul so that I will listen only to those who speak Your truth. Amen.

ADVENT—WEEK 3
Tuesday

"The Lord is close to the brokenhearted"
(Psalm 34:18).

Advent and Christmas are times when we think of the poor. Believers and unbelievers reach down into their pockets to do something for the less fortunate. Poor people are poor all year-round, but we think of them at this time. As one of those whom God has blessed with a calling to serve the poor, I am as grateful as any. Some who read this meditation are the very people who generously help me, our friars, and our sisters in our efforts to bring a little joy and relief to the poor throughout the year, but especially at the holidays.

It's interesting to ask why Advent is a special time to help the poor and less fortunate. Perhaps it is because Jesus Christ was so obviously born in the poorest circumstances, with a manger, a feeding trough for livestock, as His first crib. The poverty of His family, and in fact of His whole life, reminds us that He chose the poor. He is close to the brokenhearted, and He saves the crushed in spirit by His steadying grace and His words and example. He praises above all the poor in spirit, and He blesses those who hunger and thirst for justice.

In a life that Providence has linked with the poor, I have been aware of His blessing on the poor thousands of times. This, in fact, is the most familiar experience of my life, even more familiar than suffering itself.

In Advent, Christ reminds us: "As you did it to one of the least of these my brethren, you did it to me" (Mt 25:40). Make sure in Advent you make special efforts and real sacrifices to help the poor. Include, if you can, hands-on help as well as generous financial assistance to the point of sacrifice.

The poor are all around you: the bedridden, the very infirm and elderly, the mentally ill and lonely eccentrics, as well as the immense number of needy people found in our affluent society. Two out of every five children born in the United States are born below what the government calls the level of poverty. How appalling! Ask the Lord to open your eyes so that you may see Jesus Christ hidden in the needy around you and that you may serve him joyfully.

Prayer

Lord Jesus, open my eyes that I may see You hungry, thirsty, naked, sick, and imprisoned, that I may come to You with a generous helping hand. Let me know the joy of giving that I may become always more generous and escape from my own selfishness. Help me to find You, as the shepherds did, in the lowly stable. Amen.

ADVENT—WEEK 3
Wednesday

"Are you he who is to come, or shall we look for another?" (Luke 7:19).

Perhaps most of us, in times of trial, have posed this question in our hearts. Our prayers seem to go unheard, and at times God's providence appears to be working against us.

Facing this same situation, John the Baptist sent two of his disciples to pose this question to his kinsman, Jesus of Nazareth. He had called Jesus the Lamb of God who takes away the sins of the world, and now he found himself in the dungeon of a ridiculous but dangerous political buffoon. Could something so banal and so unjust happen to the one sent to prepare the way of the Messiah?

The incredible answer is yes. And worse was yet in store. Soon John would lose his life at the whim of a wicked woman, who has the singular distinction of being the only really wicked woman in the whole Gospel, which has a large contingent of wicked men.

The response of Jesus to John's honest questions should be one of our Advent meditations: Blessed is he who finds no stumbling-block in Me, who is not scandalized by My apparent inability to help (see Lk 7:23). While clearly indicating that He is the Messiah, the one who is to come, Jesus also lets John know what we all need to know—that God's providence does not conduct the world like a puppet show. Human beings have freedom, marred as it is by weakness and ignorance. We can do good or evil, and God will not stop us.

Long before this event, John as an unborn child leaped in his mother's womb when the unborn Messiah came to visit his home. But now evil is here. An evil far greater and more powerful than the idiotic Herod. The powers of darkness are present. This clash of good and evil will cost John his mortal life, as it will soon bring Jesus of Nazareth to His terrible death. But blessed is he who does not stumble at the apparent weakness of God, because as Christ tells us through Saint Paul: "My power is made perfect in weakness" (2 Cor 12:9).

Prayer

I have often, Lord, felt like John. I wondered where You were or if You cared to help me. It probably will happen again. Give me Your Holy Spirit that I may remain faithful like John. You have called him a blazing and shining light (see Jn 5:35). Help me, that my faith may give some little light to those around me. Amen.

ADVENT—WEEK 3
Thursday

"I will praise you, O Lord, for you have rescued me" (Psalm 30:1).

It is not unusual to experience a feeling of being abandoned by God when things go wrong. Yet we also can recall times when we feel cared for and even rescued by His providence. More likely this feeling of gratitude may come when we look back over the years and realize that some of the richest blessings we received were unrecognized at the time. The best of blessings often come wrapped up in black plastic garbage bags and are appreciated only years later.

Advent, with its memories of past Christmases, is a good time to look back. Of course there will be disappointment, wounds, and hurts—slight Christmases, as someone once called them. But as we look back, we can often see the hand of God guiding things and turning hurtful events into hidden blessings. The most painful memories are those of our own failings and sins. We realize that we have hurt others and have been unfaithful to God. Since we aspired to be disciples of Christ, we have honestly to admit to ourselves that we have failed him often.

But there is another side to these painful memories. He has not failed us. The providence of God, the teachings and grace of the Good Shepherd, and the light of the Holy Spirit have brought us out of the tangled forest of past failures into the present. What is far more important is the opportunity right now to take the next good step in the right direction, that is, on the road to holiness. In Advent, Christ says: "Follow me." But He also says: "I am rescuing you." We respond: "When will You come, Lord?" and He answers: "I am here if you welcome Me."

Prayer

Lord and Good Shepherd of my soul, how often have You rescued me and I have not even known it. Or if I have been aware of it, I have not realized the greatness of Your love and concern. Your hand was there in the darkness and danger. Continue, gentle Savior, to rescue me, and those dear to me, and the whole world because You have come to save us all. Amen.

ADVENT—WEEK 3
Friday

"The Lord is coming ... to bring peace and eternal life" (Entrance antiphon for Mass).

Peace is something we appreciate more as we get older. Youth loves excitement, challenge, and even danger. But as life goes on, we tire of agitation, and even adventure seems less attractive. We want peace.

There is a peace the world gives—an unsatisfying respite, a dull tranquillity of self-gratification, the fulfillment of dreams which leaves us more empty than before. Christ does not come to bring this peace. "I have not come to bring peace, but a sword" (Mt 10:34). Yet He is proclaimed to be the Prince of Peace. His is a different kind of kingdom and a different kind of peace. His is the peace that comes to those who open themselves every day more and more to His will. It is the peace that comes from surrendering to God's providence and from obedience to His commands. This peace cannot be lost even in the worst circumstances. It remains like a rock in the center of the soul, and when the storm breaks, it gives us a place to hold on to, an assurance that nothing else can give.

The Prince of Peace, for whom Advent prepares us, says: "My peace I give to you; not as the world gives do I give to you" (Jn 14:27). Advent invites us to sort out all the things that are really part of the peace the world gives and to separate them, at least in our thinking, from the peace of God. These things—a decent home, a pleasant neighborhood, tranquil family relationships—are all good. They remain blessings as long as they do not become our final goal, our ultimate happiness. Then they would become lies because they cannot last. We need to accept these blessings knowing that they all have strings attached. They will all come to an end. If we let him, the Prince of Peace will teach us to seek in His will the peace that the world can neither give nor take away.

Prayer

Lord, give me Your peace. Give me the grace to place in Your hands all the good things I have in life, even my loved ones. They are, after all, Your gifts. And prepare me for that one great gift which cannot be taken away—Your peace. May all whom I love and care about come to Your peace. May we love one another in Your peace, never to be separated again, because Your peace is our everlasting life. Amen.

Note: The order of these meditations is based on a full four weeks of Advent, with Christmas being a full week after the fourth Sunday. We begin today the seven individual days in the liturgical calendar, each of which has its own Mass and Office. If Advent is shorter than four full weeks (which it usually is), you would begin using these meditations on December 17. The theme of the antiphons used at Evening Prayer, or Vespers, is woven into each meditation. Because each of the prayers begins with the exclamation "O," they have traditionally been referred to as the O antiphons.

> *"Jacob was the father of Joseph, the husband of Mary. It was to her that Jesus who is called the Messiah was born" (Matthew 1:16).*

The Gospel of the genealogy of Christ is often puzzling to those who come to weekday Mass before Christmas and hear it read out loud. Even in Christian denominations that center everything on the Bible, this is not the most popular text, and in fact many Christians have never heard it read aloud. Admittedly, it is a challenge for someone who must read it aloud. On the other hand, in many countries where traditional cultures still survive, as in Africa, it makes all the sense in the world. While they might not go back this many generations, many Africans can give you their own lengthy genealogy.

The purpose of this list in the Gospel would have been perfectly obvious to early Hebrew Christians. It roots the Messiah in the very center of Jewish history, although His immediate ancestors on Joseph's side were apparently humble people. In fact, he was born among those we would call peasants, or people of the land.

There are many things to learn from this fact. One example is the humility of God. But today we should focus on one thing: the Incarnation really happened. It's not a myth. Take away the magic of the winter holiday and even the tender sentiment of the Christian devotion to the holy Infant, and you have the core that is absolute and astonishing. The Incarnation calls for adoration and loving acceptance. The mysterious and almighty mind that made all things from the incredibly gigantic universe to the infinitesimal gene and arranged these things so that rational beings could live and grow and hope to live forever—that Wisdom comes as a human child.

Let us adore.

O Wisdom, You came forth from the mouth of the Most High, and reaching from beginning to end, You ordered all things mightily and sweetly. Come, and teach us the way of prudence!

Prayer

God of wisdom and power, God of humility, who make the stars and the atoms and bring them into harmony, give me your wise and holy Spirit that I may bow my whole being in adoration to the coming of Your Son, called the son of Joseph. Amen.

ADVENT—WEEK 4
The Fourth Sunday — December 18

"The Holy Spirit will come upon you, and the power of the Most High will overshadow you; hence the holy offspring to be born will be called Son of God" (Luke 1:35).

If you have little faith, you may find yourself tempted to explain away any and all of the miracles surrounding the birth of our Savior. Any honest reading of the Gospel accounts will make clear even to the unbeliever that the direct action of divine power is essential to the fabric of this account. Today's O antiphon evokes the image of the burning bush, which, because it was a sign of God's power and presence, was not destroyed by the fire. Many saints have taken this image of the burning bush as a symbol of the perpetual virginity of Mary.

Woven through the account of Jesus' conception and birth is the belief of those who participated (and of those who knew from first-hand accounts) that the outstretched hand of God was there. Once the possibility of the direct action of God's power is accepted, as it must be as an object of belief, then the Gospel accounts make perfect sense. How else could the eternal Word of God, equal to the Father in all things, become man except by God's direct action?

Some may ask, "Why a virgin birth?" The obvious answer is, "Ask God." It is easy for doubt to enter here. It is even easier for mind games to take over. Some believe, but with smoke and mirrors.

As we approach the festal commemoration of the Messiah's birth, we need to foster a habit of mind that people find difficult. We need to reject quite consciously the rationalist prejudice that the human mind can comprehend everything in heaven and on earth. We are surrounded by natural mysteries, like gravity, time, and matter. We accept them and go on. Why not the mystery of grace, the mystery beyond the natural world?

While it is unwise to attribute motives to God's actions, one can at least meditate on the reason for Christ's coming. The mystery of the human body and soul assumed by the eternal Son of God at the time of the Incarnation requires faith in an absolutely inexplicable act of God's power. It is the grace of all graces. How better could human beings come to appreciate the mystery of the Incarnation than to acknowledge that His mother conceived Him entirely by divine power and not by any human intervention?

O Adonai and Ruler of the house of Israel, You appeared to Moses in the fire of the burning bush, and on Mount Sinai gave him Your law. Come, and with an outstretched arm redeem us!

Prayer

O Holy Spirit, fire of the burning bush, Your presence and action did not coerce the Virgin but freely made her mother of the Son of God. Speak in our hearts with the same divine power with which You spoke to Moses so that we may believe and come to salvation. Amen.

ADVENT—WEEK 4
Monday — December 19

"God ... will go before him ... to turn the hearts of the fathers to the children, and the rebellious to the wisdom of the just and to prepare for the Lord a people well disposed" (Luke 1:16-17).

The words of the angelic messenger to Zechariah, in announcing the coming birth of John the Baptist, are filled with authority and show us something very important about the coming of Christ Himself. It is an apparent paradox that Christ comes to give us unconditional salvation by His life and death. He is our Savior. But we need to do our own part. John has his task, and those who hear him—the hard-hearted fathers, the rebellious, and the undisposed—are called to change. John can convert them, but only if they are willing to be changed.

The words of the angel contain an issue that comes up over and over again. Confusion reigns on one side from those who think that they can save themselves, and on the other side from those who think that they can be utterly passive. The simple fact is we must decide to change, and we must do all that is necessary for our human minds and wills to be converted. Salvation comes from God, but it is a two-way street. Our hearts must become compassionate, our rebellious attitudes must become wise and just, and we must be open and well disposed to hear the Good News.

Obviously we cannot do these things by ourselves. We need God's grace even to make us want to cooperate with Him. But the mystery is that God cannot make us change if we are unwilling to do so. Because of the freedom He has given us, we can and often do rebel. Advent calls us to renew our desire to change, to remain submissive before His divine majesty, and to accept His deliverance.

O Root of Jesse, You stand as an ensign for mankind; before You kings shall keep silence, and to You all nations shall have recourse. Come, save us, and do not delay.

Prayer

Lord Jesus Christ, You were born of the central stock of the chosen people, the root of Jesse. But You came to save us all. May the rulers of our own time fall to silence before You, and may You hear us, the Gentiles, as we beg You to deliver us from evil. Amen.

ADVENT—WEEK 4
Tuesday — December 20

"I am the handmaid of the Lord; let it be done unto to me according to thy word" (Luke 1:38).

These are the most important words ever spoken by a mortal human being. Only the words of Christ himself can be more important than these words, which are often called Mary's *fiat*, that is, "let it be done." On behalf of the whole human race, Mary says yes to God.

How much there is for us to learn from her consent. Fourteen hundred years later inquisitors would ask Joan of Arc, "Why would God choose a little peasant girl?" Her response is powerful in its simplicity and reminds us somewhat of the mystery of the Annunciation to Mary. "I suppose He wanted to choose a little peasant girl," Joan said. Bernadette Soubirous would answer the same question in the same way centuries later. It is not wise for mortal men to attempt to read God's mind, but we can say at least that He wanted to show that His grace and salvation did not depend on what humans deserve.

The angel's greeting, "Highly favored one" or "full of grace," shows that God had very clearly prepared His handmaid for her task. This was no accident or random event of nature. He comes, He opens, and no one shuts.

And yet, how moving and fitting it is that Mary must consent. The world was lost by a young woman's decision, and it was saved in the same way. At least since the second century Eve and Mary have been seen as mysteriously related. The early Christian writers called Mary the new Eve and her Son the new Adam. Our meditations now move us into the most profound spiritual mysteries. The focus turns from what we do to respond to God to a contemplation of what He has done for us.

O Key of David and Scepter of the house of Israel: You open and no one closes; You close and no one opens. Come, and deliver from the chains of prison those who sit in darkness and in the shadow of death.

Prayer

Lord God, open my being to the wonder of Your grace and let me never again take lightly the mystery of salvation. Open, and let no one close my heart to the mystery of Your Emmanuel and His Mother, whom You chose and who in awe and obedience responded by saying yes to Your messenger. Amen.

"Blessed is she who has trusted that the Lord's words to her would be fulfilled" (Luke 1:45).

How often the faithful Christian has read these words, but their significance can be lost as the drama of the Nativity unfolds. Why is Mary blessed? Because she has trusted in the word of God. Her consent to the heavenly messenger, her willingness to take on her young shoulders the burden of the glorious Messiah and the Man of Sorrows as the prophets had foretold is all built on her act of trust. And this trust did not stop with the virginal conception of Christ. She would have to trust God when, at her baby's birth, she found no other place in which to place Him than a manger, a feeding trough. She would trust when she was forced to leave her homeland and all that was familiar and flee to Egypt, where she knew no one. She would trust again during her three-day search for her lost boy, finding Him at last in the temple. She would trust on the roads of Galilee and on the way of sorrow to Calvary. Still she would trust as He cried out in His last agony and then died. "Blessed is she who has trusted."

The whole secret of the spiritual life is trust. Do you want to grow in faith and the love of God? Then trust Him. We trust when it is easy; we must trust when it is hard. In fact, trust is an act of the virtue of hope. Like faith and charity, this kind of hope can be given only by God's grace. Our heart is to be open to receive this gift and to put it into practice by an act of trustful surrender. We must trust when there is a bright star overhead and when the darkness covers the earth at noon. As we prepare to leave this world at the end of our lives, may we see the rising Dawn before us. Let us pray that then we will know even beyond the certitude of faith that they are blessed who trust in the word of God.

O Rising Dawn, Radiance of the Light eternal and Sun of Justice; come, and enlighten those who sit in darkness and in the shadow of death.

Prayer

Lord Jesus, You have been my light for a long time, and I am forever grateful. But give me the grace to open the eyes of my soul ever more and to turn from the shadows so that my life may become simply a reflection of Your light. Amen.

ADVENT—WEEK 4
Thursday — December 22

"His mercy is on those who fear him from generation to generation" (Luke 1:50).

The Gospel of this day is Mary's song of praise, a marvelous New Testament psalm of thanksgiving and joy that God has lifted up the lowly. There are those, of course, who question whether Mary said these words or similar words. While the questioners must admit that they were not there at the Visitation and that Luke either spoke to the Mother of Jesus or to those who knew her well, we can accept these words as a gift of the Holy Spirit. They are inspired words of revelation given to the Christian people so that we may know the sentiments of the second most mysterious person who ever lived and that we may joyfully learn from them.

There is a whole treasury of powerful and beautiful thoughts in the Magnificat, or Song of Mary. We take one thought for today. "His mercy is on those who fear Him," that is, on those who reverence Him and His holiness. The world we live in has almost no reverence for beauty, for human love, for the family, for life itself, or for God. But despite all this irreverence, especially in the media, there is a constant stream of unforeseen reverence from unexpected sources. Those with no religious training at all or those whose own being has not been revered will suddenly turn and become the most humble and docile servants of God. Someplace within them the grace of God has found a trace of reverence and awe, and they have received mercy. The devout and the believing become aware of this transformation, often enough with surprise but also with wonder and joy. We often overlook entirely the beautiful and simple faith of the very poor and downtrodden.

Although the Virgin was most sinless, she was poor and, by her own words, "lowly." She speaks in this canticle for the hungry and the humble. We need to listen to these words. I see them as a preface to the sermon her Son will give three decades later on the mountainside in Galilee. May we be among those who reverence His holiness and power so that we may receive His mercy, which we might need more than we are aware.

O King of the Gentiles and the Desired of all, you are the cornerstone that binds two into one. Come, and save poor man whom you fashioned out of clay.

Prayer

Lord Jesus, all our true joy must come from You. We are the poor and the lowly too. We have no true and lasting joy without You. O King of the nations, who is born, lives, and dies in a poor corner of the land of Israel, be my king always. Amen.

"What then will this child be? Was not the hand of the Lord upon him?" (Luke 1:66).

One must say John the Baptist illustrates very well what it means to be a disciple of Christ. To be a follower, or disciple, of any human being, however virtuous or charismatic, is very different from being a follower of Christ. Even we who aspire to be disciples of Christ can follow another of His disciples who leads and supports us on the way to Christ. It may be a bishop or a preacher or a founder of some deeply spiritual movement, and this person becomes a guide to us. We learn from them, are inspired by them, or if they lived long ago, we are guided by their writings and example. It could be Saint Francis or Saint Ignatius or John Wesley. But to be a follower of Christ is essentially different. To be His follower, the Lord's hand must rest upon you. Saint Augustine tells us: "We did not choose the Way; the Way chose us."

Although Mary herself must be called the first disciple, John's discipleship is more like our own. He is pulled outside himself. He does things one would not expect from a boy of the priestly caste. He lives in the desert. He preaches and baptizes as an act of repentance. But in prison he questions Jesus: "Are you he who is to come, or shall we look for another?" (Lk 7:19). The mystery of God's humility and the Messiah's apparent weakness in the face of wickedness cause John to question. But he does not surrender. He is not overcome. Why? Because the hand of the Lord is upon him.

Face it. The hand of the Lord is upon you. If you have read these meditations this far, it is hard for me to believe that you are not a disciple. So am I. Hopefully we know our weaknesses and limitations very well. We can fall and fail like the apostles. Like Judas, we can completely lose everything. But nonetheless the Lord's hand is upon us. It is our calling to be loyal to that vocation, to humble ourselves beneath the mighty hand of God.

O Emmanuel, our King and Lawgiver, the Expected of nations and their Savior: Come, and save us, O Lord our God!

Prayer

Lord Jesus, You guide us by Your laws, laws of mind and heart. We rely on Your grace: do not let us depart from Your way. If we move away from You, from Your mighty hand, we are lost. Keep Your hand upon us, O Lord, and remind us that Your hand is both wounded and glorified. Amen.

ADVENT—WEEK 4
December 24 — Christmas Eve

"He has raised up for us a mighty savior born of the house of his servant David" (Luke 1:69).

Most of us can remember Christmas Eve as a day of anticipation and even of a bit of worry. Would we get our Christmas presents the coming night? Usually there was something we wanted—a toy or a game we had seen in a shop window. If you went to a religious school, there was the anticipation of looking forward to the beautiful services with many a well-practiced Christmas carol. If you were an altar boy, as I was, there was a fresh linen surplice and a red cassock, just like a bishop's.

I always felt sorry for the Jewish kids in our neighborhood. They had no lights outside their houses and—imagine!—no Christmas tree. I was glad that the celebration of Hanukkah became popular, but it never got near Christmas.

But if I may say so respectfully, Christmas Eve reminds me of the Jewish people. It is a day of expectation, which recalls the devout Jews who are waiting patiently and prayerfully for the Messiah. I heard the Hasidim singing a joyous song at the Temple wall: "Be pure, be pure. Tomorrow He will come." I spoke to them, and they were very serious about the Messiah possibly coming the next day.

The canticle of Zachary in the Gospel for Christmas Eve is really the hymn of praise at the end of Advent, a time that symbolizes the long centuries during which the Jewish people waited. When you read this hymn, the counterpoint of Mary's song of praise, you can feel the joy of the Jewish people at the coming of the Messiah. Zachary's song is a hymn of triumph over the power of evil and darkness that had harrowed the devout children of Abraham for so long. The infant John in his father's arms is to be the last of the prophets to prepare immediately the way of the Lord.

Why do the Jewish people not know about the Messiah? It's not my business to ask. The Promised One Himself said, "No one can come to Me unless the Father who sent Me draws him" (Jn 6:44). I have always had great respect for the faith and reverence of devout Jews. I grew up with many Jewish neighbors who observed the Sabbath more piously than we Christians observed Sunday. I put my Jewish friends completely in the hands of the "Dayspring from on high."[2]

It's the Christians I am worried about! Have we prepared the way of the Lord? Have we listened carefully to the last of the prophets, John? Do we, to use Zachary's term, have a knowledge of salvation for the forgiveness of sins?

Tonight will be a night of mysterious gifts, much more mysterious than the toys found under the Christmas tree in the early morning. Tonight He comes to remind us that every day, every hour He is here for us, saying, "Come to Me."

Prayer

O Messiah, Anointed One of God, send Your grace on Your people. Give Your Holy Spirit not only to Christians but also to Jews and all other people who seek to find and please God. Come to all Your sheep in Your own mysterious way. Do not let any heart remain in the dark. Shine on us all who dwell in darkness and in the shadow of death. Amen.

CHRISTMAS SEASON
December 25 — Christmas Day

"A child is born to us, a Son is given to us"
(Isaiah 9:6).

Jesus Christ was born to give Himself away because the life of the Trinity, the three divine Persons, is one of total self-giving, of love in the highest and purest meaning of that word. When we were children, the smiling, sweet image of the baby Jesus surely was meant to take away any unworthy fear of God. The little figure was to tell us that the God of the Gospels was not a fearful judge. And so Christmas should be a joyous, warm, and friendly day.

But the figure of the Christ Child is not the whole picture by any means. The Child was, in reality, among the poorest of the poor, laid in a manger. He was soon to be a political refugee fleeing a brutal tyrant. He was to live a life of essential misunderstanding. No one—not even His Mother—could entirely understand what it meant for Him to be "about [His] Father's business." He would live His public life almost completely surrounded by people, begging people, insistent people, demanding the help of heaven. Paradoxically, He was completely given to people and their needs and yet in the depths of His soul He was entirely apart. "I and the Father are one" (Jn 10:30).

In a few decades the Child of Bethlehem will stand at the absolute pinnacle of the conflict between good and evil. His shoulders will bear all that burden. He will be crushed by the weight of the world's sins. He is the only Person of whom it can be said that He was born to die. He knew that it was to be His calling.

How does one cope with the real mystery of Christmas? It can be the saddest of days for many people. Some are very alone; some feel deserted or neglected. Some are isolated but will go off among the poor who have much fun as they open the Christmas baskets given to them. Perhaps the loneliest person in the world is a man sitting in his own living room surrounded by his family and no one will really speak to him. And he knows it's his own fault.

The answer on Christmas Day is to give and forgive. Spend the day for others in good works and prayer. Give yourself away, and if there is no one to give yourself to, pray for those you care about even if they seem not to care about you. Christmas is a day for giving. We should think about it that way from the time we are young until we are very old. A smile and a prayer can be our gifts of the Magi to the Christ Child.

Prayer

Lord Jesus Christ, let me live for You today and give myself to all I meet, especially those in need. Whatever they need—a smile, a helping hand, a meal, forgiveness—help me to get out of the prison of myself and to follow You, who came from beyond the stars to give Your love away. Amen.

CHRISTMAS SEASON
December 26 — Saint Stephen, martyr

"I see the heavens opened and the Son of man standing at the right hand of God" (Acts 7:56).

If the days before Christmas and the feast day itself have lifted up our minds and hearts to the transcendent beauty of God's love for us, the account of the brutal stoning and martyrdom of the young disciple Stephen brings us startlingly back to earth. The song of the angels, "Peace on earth," almost seems like a painful irony as we read of his martyrdom. Why does the Church break the beauty of this sacred season with the commemoration of the first martyr? Our good sense tells us that this is more than a jarring coincidence. What we encounter already is the clash between good and evil, between infinite goodness and the darkest, deepest evil. Stephen's death reminds us that Jesus has come to take on all evil, to destroy it by love and forgiveness. Of course, this conflict is an unfathomable mystery or, better, the coming together of a number of mysteries. First of all there is the overwhelming light of God's love and the redemption. But there is also the mystery of evil, impenetrable not because of its light but as a result of its darkness. Whenever good and evil come into contact with each other, great suffering is bound to happen on all sides.

There is the further irony that those who killed Stephen thought they were paying homage to God. They were avenging blasphemy and fighting what they thought to be polytheism in the midst of the Hebrew world. They thought that they were doing good. The mystery of this conflict and tragic misunderstanding, which would be repeated innumerable times, is symbolized by the dark brooding figure of Saul of Tarsus, an approving witness to the death of the first martyr. Who would have thought at that moment that (God's) "power is made perfect in weakness" (2 Cor 12:9) and that "where sin abounded, grace did more abound" (Rom 5:20)? Saul, soon to be called Paul, would write these words celebrating the good news that the mercy of God revealed in the Christ Child could change evil into good by love.

Prayer

O Lord Jesus Christ, let us have some experience of Your inner presence, as Stephen saw You at the hour of his martyrdom. Let us know that You are with us while remaining at the right hand of the Father. When the sky is dark and we are in the grip of apprehension, open the heavens to our souls so that we may see that You are always with us. Amen.

CHRISTMAS SEASON
December 27 — Saint John, evangelist

"And the Word was made flesh and dwelt among us" (John 1:14).

The Church gives to the author of the great Gospel of the divinity of Christ the honor of a feast day just after Christmas. All of the Gospels proclaim Christ's divinity, but none so eloquently and repeatedly as the Gospel of John. One might say that this small book of some twenty-two thousand words in English is the foundation stone of Christian spirituality. Christ's words in this Gospel reveal in the most profound way that, "He who sees me sees the Father also" (14:9) and that "If anyone keeps my word, my Father will love him, and we will come to him and make our home with him" (14:23). In this Gospel, God is referred to as Father almost a hundred times. Along with the epistles of Saint Paul, this Gospel presents the whole foundation of Christian life as a life lived in union with Jesus Christ in the mystery of grace.

We have meditated already on the mystery of the Incarnate Word. Today we logically move to the mystery of our lives united with Him. This thought is so overwhelming that you can think about its meaning for the rest of your life and still learn more and more beautiful things each day. The Word of God came so that we might participate in the eternity of God. That is why we have the hope of eternal life. All human beings have at least a hidden hope that they will not fade at death into the darkness of oblivion. The Christian, above all others, knows that the spark of divine life in the human soul is not a false promise but the sign of a call to salvation. But how? How can flesh that is so vulnerable, so timebound, so caught in the stream of time leading to death—how can flesh hope to live forever? John gives the answer in the marvelous prologue, or introduction, to his Gospel. He tells us that Christ gives to all who receive Him and believe in His name the right to become "children of God ... born ... of God" (1:12-13).

Prayer

Holy Spirit, come to us again and again. Show us more deeply everyday what it is to be a child of God, a sister or brother of the Lord by adoption. Teach us to honor our human nature raised up to eternal promise by the newborn Messiah. Enlighten us so that we and those we love may in fact be born of the Father. Amen.

Me" (Mt 10:12). Jesus gave this challenge long before anyone knew that He Himself was going to be crucified. His hearers all knew what it meant for a condemned man to carry his cross. Our way of the cross is not likely to be as dramatic as Saint Thomas'. He lived through months of conflict and weeks of dreadful anticipation of a death that was likely to come at any time. Each of us needs to ask the Holy Spirit for the gift of courage when the time of trial comes and the wisdom to know what to do.

The thoughts of these days seem somber and dark for Christmas week. But ultimately they are not. They are the most joyous of messages. Christ's coming will bring victory over evil and death to all who welcome Him into their lives.

Prayer

Lord Jesus, give me and those dear to me the fullness of Your Holy Spirit that I may be loyal to Your truth and that I may overcome fear and put my life and all its hopes safely into Your hands. Amen.

CHRISTMAS SEASON
December 28 — The Holy Innocents

"Rachel weeping for her children and refusing comfort because they were no more" (Matthew 2:18).

If the death of Stephen is a startling contrast to the joy of Christ's birth, then today's message seems a complete contradiction of the whole account of the coming of the Prince of Peace. At least this commemoration of the murder of all the infant boys of Bethlehem could have been placed weeks after Christmas, especially after the Epiphany. Why is it here amid Christmas carols and family visits in the middle of Christmas week? I think it is because the Christian must be prepared to have the good news of Christ challenged, not only by the unbelief of men but also by the darkest possible events of life. This sorrowful day is a reminder of all the persecutions, all the tryannies, all the atrocious evils that can and will happen in the centuries ahead. The coming of the Prince of Peace did not stop criminal abominations like Auschwitz, or even natural disasters like earthquakes and tornadoes. By placing this dark day so soon after Christmas, it would seem that the Church wants to make very clear to us that the sign of Christ will not be the star of Bethlehem or even the Good Shepherd's staff. His sign will be the mysterious cross.

The cries of slaughtered children, called so poetically the Holy Innocents, echo loudly through our time. For those deeply committed to the cause of life this is a day of pilgrimage and prayerful reparation and fervent petition to end the slaughter of children in our own time. In Bethlehem there could have been no more than a few dozen baby boys under two years of age. The ranks have swelled to tens of millions of babies legally killed and dismembered in a way that eerily reminds us of the medieval painting of that terrible event. The Holy Innocents call to Christians over the centuries to raise their voices against evil and injustice. Christ's peace is not a passive state of dreamy harmony that one sees in living-room paintings. Christ's peace is the victory prize in a relentless conflict lasting until the end of the world. But the believer has hope in the ultimate victory—that the holy innocents of our time join in that great procession when each of them will be given "a white robe and told to wait a little longer, until the number of their fellow servants and brothers who were killed is completed" (Rv 6:11). And then they will shout out in a loud voice: "Salvation belongs to our God who sits upon the throne, and to the Lamb!" (Rv 7:10).

Prayer

Lord Jesus, keep me always waiting, always looking forward to the day when You "will wipe away every tear" from our eyes. Then "there will be no more death, or mourning, or crying, or pain" (Rv 21:4). Amen.

CHRISTMAS SEASON
December 29 — Saint Thomas Becket, marty

"The good shepherd lays down His life for th sheep" (John 10:11).

The trilogy of martyrdom after Christmas is completed by the of this twelfth-century archbishop of Canterbury. For English-sp Christians many elements of the Christmas celebration were E in origin—many of the traditional hymns and carols, and stori Dickens' *A Christmas Carol* with Bob Cratchit and Tiny Tim. always seemed proper to me that our liturgical week should i the heroic English bishop who died this day in 1170, bravely ing the rights of the Church. Again we see that the Prince o comes to bring a sword—literally, in Becket's case. One can still spot in the incredibly beautiful cathedral of Canterbury wh archbishop was struck down by the sword by the henchmen who called himself a Christian king. It is worth mentioni Becket's name is known to millions who could not tell you th of the king. He was not necessarily worse than many others, king was pulled into the fierce tides of the conflict between g evil. It is said that he repented, maybe even sincerely.

Saint Thomas was a repentant sinner himself. He surp king, his old drinking buddy, by becoming a real follower of Saint Thomas' message is valuable for all who want to dee faith and make a new start, a more authentic attempt at l Christians. We have to pay the price.

"If anyone will come after Me, he must take up his cross a

CHRISTMAS SEASON
The Holy Family
(Sunday following Christmas Day)[3]

"An angel of the Lord appeared in a dream to Joseph and said, 'Get up, take the child and His mother, and flee to Egypt' (Matthew 2:13).

Although the ancient Church recognized good reasons to think of the family into which Christ was born as including the children of Joseph—the stepbrothers and -sisters of Jesus—Christian devotion in modern times has focused simply on Jesus, Mary, and Joseph. With all due respect to the possible stepbrothers and -sisters of Jesus, they would fit into our thinking as part of the large cast of people who are in the great drama of salvation. If they existed, they can be seen in a way similar to the shepherds, the women of Galilee, and the crowds on Palm Sunday. The brothers of Jesus are quoted as saying that He had gone mad (see Mark 3:21). One hopes that at least these were kinsmen and not members of the holy household.

The touching picture of the Nativity, the flight into Egypt, and the events in the temple when He was twelve years old show Jesus in a complex relationship to His family. He is subject to Mary and Joseph. He appears to work a miracle at Cana when His Mother importunes him; He speaks with loving care from the Cross to His Mother. But there is a distance too. "Who is my mother? Who are my brothers?... Whoever does the will of my heavenly Father is brother and sister and mother to me" (Mt 12:48–50). His Mother would not have disagreed.

She knew that we must prefer God to mother and father and all things. Of all human beings, she did prefer God above all. Even when she stood at the foot of the Cross, she sacrificed her own human love for the flesh she had brought into this world.

The Christian is called to be a loving person. Christianity is a religion of love of God and love of all others in God. "God is love, and he who abides in love abides in God, and God abides in him" (1 Jn 4:16). "Having loved His own who were in the world, He loved them to the end" (Jn 13:1). We all love on many levels. We love because we need; we love because we share. We can love those who need us because they need us, and we can love because we want to follow the Gospel. We can try with God's help to love even our enemies. A family may give us an experience of every kind of love listed above, but one thing is for sure. If we have a family, even only one other person whom we love, we must learn to forgive. If we do not define forgiveness too strictly or morally but rather as a psychological phenomenon, letting hurts go by, accepting what we do not understand, what may have been hurtful to us even if no wrongdoing occurred, then perhaps we can say that Mary and Joseph had to forgive the mysterious person who lived with them. The frightening days of searching for the Christ Child in Jerusalem are a good case in point.

Don't be shocked at the idea of forgiving God. Not that we forgive God theologically. Such an idea would be absurd. But haven't we all said to God, Why? Why did You let that happen? It can be a banged-in fender on our car or the painful death of a loved one. Our questioning can lead to a very helpful conclusion. Belong to a family of any kind, belong really even to your parish or community or circle of friends, and you will have to forgive. This is perhaps one of the reasons why Christ did not emerge into human history as a full-grown man. He was born into a family so that He could experience what we experience, so that He could ask us to forgive those who trespass against us.

Prayer

Lord Jesus, Your family life was very private. We get a glimpse of it only here and there. For most of us family life is quite private too. Private joys and private hurts. Help us, Lord, to love and to learn from Your example. We also must sadly leave what we love. In a mysterious way You left Your family of eternal bliss, the holy Trinity, and came here for us. You understand. Amen.

"She gave thanks to God and spoke about the Child to all who looked forward to the deliverance of Jerusalem" (Luke 2:38).

It is one of the blessings of religious history, in contrast to most other historical accounts, that it often tells us about the "little people." The vast majority of people at any time are on the sidelines. Their lives and even their deaths are directed by the very few who make the decisions that are recorded in world history. Thank God the Gospels are filled with little people. Anna, the focus of today's Gospel, is one of the first people we meet after the shepherds. Her walk through salvation history is a tender and revealing moment.

Anna, whose name means mercy or grace, was one of a known class of older widows who lived in the temple and served it both domestically and spiritually. I have seen such women with their tiny little bedrolls and few eating utensils living and working in the Buddhist temples of the Orient. They seemed largely unaware of the throngs of visitors and tourists; the temple was after all their home. They were so thin that they reminded me of the sparrows that one sometimes sees nesting inside great buildings.

Anna was eighty-four, an advanced age in those days, and never left the temple, spending her time in fasting and prayer. Being a prophetess, she, like Simeon, recognized that the baby was the one sent to deliver God's people. Also like Simeon, she saw with her eyes the salvation prepared by God.

We learn two things from Anna. The first is never to overlook the little people or to pass them by because they are not in the mainstream. Any intelligent person knows that the mainstream is usually going in the wrong direction and that the movers and shakers are almost always moving and shaking the wrong things. Recall Herod and Pilate. The really important people are those God counts as important.

The second thing to be learned from Anna is that we need to listen carefully to souls who are close to God. Recently a Cardinal archbishop with many years of education and experience told me that he learned most of the things he ever knew from holy old ladies. (Holy old men are more rare, but they are around.) Open your eyes. You may have been speaking to an Anna or a Simeon for years and never realized it.

Prayer

Holy Spirit, give me the grace to stop and listen to those who are close to You—far closer than I am. Help me to discern those who are old and wise and even now await our deliverance by the Son of God. Let me not be a fool like those who laughed at Anna and Simeon. Teach me to listen when You speak to me through those who, by grace and prayer, have received You with faith and love. Amen.

CHRISTMAS SEASON
December 28 — The Holy Innocents

"Rachel weeping for her children and refusing comfort because they were no more" (Matthew 2:18).

If the death of Stephen is a startling contrast to the joy of Christ's birth, then today's message seems a complete contradiction of the whole account of the coming of the Prince of Peace. At least this commemoration of the murder of all the infant boys of Bethlehem could have been placed weeks after Christmas, especially after the Epiphany. Why is it here amid Christmas carols and family visits in the middle of Christmas week? I think it is because the Christian must be prepared to have the good news of Christ challenged, not only by the unbelief of men but also by the darkest possible events of life. This sorrowful day is a reminder of all the persecutions, all the tryannies, all the atrocious evils that can and will happen in the centuries ahead. The coming of the Prince of Peace did not stop criminal abominations like Auschwitz, or even natural disasters like earthquakes and tornadoes. By placing this dark day so soon after Christmas, it would seem that the Church wants to make very clear to us that the sign of Christ will not be the star of Bethlehem or even the Good Shepherd's staff. His sign will be the mysterious cross.

The cries of slaughtered children, called so poetically the Holy Innocents, echo loudly through our time. For those deeply committed to the cause of life this is a day of pilgrimage and prayerful reparation and fervent petition to end the slaughter of children in our own time. In Bethlehem there could have been no more than a few dozen baby boys under two years of age. The ranks have swelled to tens of millions of babies legally killed and dismembered in a way that eerily reminds us of the medieval painting of that terrible event. The Holy Innocents call to Christians over the centuries to raise their voices against evil and injustice. Christ's peace is not a passive state of dreamy harmony that one sees in living-room paintings. Christ's peace is the victory prize in a relentless conflict lasting until the end of the world. But the believer has hope in the ultimate victory—that the holy innocents of our time join in that great procession when each of them will be given "a white robe and told to wait a little longer, until the number of their fellow servants and brothers who were killed is completed" (Rv 6:11). And then they will shout out in a loud voice: "Salvation belongs to our God who sits upon the throne, and to the Lamb!" (Rv 7:10).

Prayer

Lord Jesus, keep me always waiting, always looking forward to the day when You "will wipe away every tear" from our eyes. Then "there will be no more death, or mourning, or crying, or pain" (Rv 21:4). Amen.

CHRISTMAS SEASON
December 29 — Saint Thomas Becket, martyr

"The good shepherd lays down His life for the sheep" (John 10:11).

The trilogy of martyrdom after Christmas is completed by the death of this twelfth-century archbishop of Canterbury. For English-speaking Christians many elements of the Christmas celebration were English in origin—many of the traditional hymns and carols, and stories like Dickens' *A Christmas Carol* with Bob Cratchit and Tiny Tim. It has always seemed proper to me that our liturgical week should include the heroic English bishop who died this day in 1170, bravely defending the rights of the Church. Again we see that the Prince of Peace comes to bring a sword—literally, in Becket's case. One can still see the spot in the incredibly beautiful cathedral of Canterbury where the archbishop was struck down by the sword by the henchmen of one who called himself a Christian king. It is worth mentioning that Becket's name is known to millions who could not tell you the name of the king. He was not necessarily worse than many others, but this king was pulled into the fierce tides of the conflict between good and evil. It is said that he repented, maybe even sincerely.

Saint Thomas was a repentant sinner himself. He surprised the king, his old drinking buddy, by becoming a real follower of Christ. Saint Thomas' message is valuable for all who want to deepen their faith and make a new start, a more authentic attempt at being real Christians. We have to pay the price.

"If anyone will come after Me, he must take up his cross and follow

Me" (Mt 10:12). Jesus gave this challenge long before anyone knew that He Himself was going to be crucified. His hearers all knew what it meant for a condemned man to carry his cross. Our way of the cross is not likely to be as dramatic as Saint Thomas'. He lived through months of conflict and weeks of dreadful anticipation of a death that was likely to come at any time. Each of us needs to ask the Holy Spirit for the gift of courage when the time of trial comes and the wisdom to know what to do.

The thoughts of these days seem somber and dark for Christmas week. But ultimately they are not. They are the most joyous of messages. Christ's coming will bring victory over evil and death to all who welcome Him into their lives.

Prayer

Lord Jesus, give me and those dear to me the fullness of Your Holy Spirit that I may be loyal to Your truth and that I may overcome fear and put my life and all its hopes safely into Your hands. Amen.

CHRISTMAS SEASON
The Holy Family
(Sunday following Christmas Day)[3]

"An angel of the Lord appeared in a dream to Joseph and said, 'Get up, take the child and His mother, and flee to Egypt' (Matthew 2:13).

Although the ancient Church recognized good reasons to think of the family into which Christ was born as including the children of Joseph—the stepbrothers and -sisters of Jesus—Christian devotion in modern times has focused simply on Jesus, Mary, and Joseph. With all due respect to the possible stepbrothers and -sisters of Jesus, they would fit into our thinking as part of the large cast of people who are in the great drama of salvation. If they existed, they can be seen in a way similar to the shepherds, the women of Galilee, and the crowds on Palm Sunday. The brothers of Jesus are quoted as saying that He had gone mad (see Mark 3:21). One hopes that at least these were kinsmen and not members of the holy household.

The touching picture of the Nativity, the flight into Egypt, and the events in the temple when He was twelve years old show Jesus in a complex relationship to His family. He is subject to Mary and Joseph. He appears to work a miracle at Cana when His Mother importunes him; He speaks with loving care from the Cross to His Mother. But there is a distance too. "Who is my mother? Who are my brothers?... Whoever does the will of my heavenly Father is brother and sister and mother to me" (Mt 12:48–50). His Mother would not have disagreed.

She knew that we must prefer God to mother and father and all things. Of all human beings, she did prefer God above all. Even when she stood at the foot of the Cross, she sacrificed her own human love for the flesh she had brought into this world.

The Christian is called to be a loving person. Christianity is a religion of love of God and love of all others in God. "God is love, and he who abides in love abides in God, and God abides in him" (1 Jn 4:16). "Having loved His own who were in the world, He loved them to the end" (Jn 13:1). We all love on many levels. We love because we need; we love because we share. We can love those who need us because they need us, and we can love because we want to follow the Gospel. We can try with God's help to love even our enemies. A family may give us an experience of every kind of love listed above, but one thing is for sure. If we have a family, even only one other person whom we love, we must learn to forgive. If we do not define forgiveness too strictly or morally but rather as a psychological phenomenon, letting hurts go by, accepting what we do not understand, what may have been hurtful to us even if no wrongdoing occurred, then perhaps we can say that Mary and Joseph had to forgive the mysterious person who lived with them. The frightening days of searching for the Christ Child in Jerusalem are a good case in point.

Don't be shocked at the idea of forgiving God. Not that we forgive God theologically. Such an idea would be absurd. But haven't we all said to God, Why? Why did You let that happen? It can be a banged-in fender on our car or the painful death of a loved one. Our questioning can lead to a very helpful conclusion. Belong to a family of any kind, belong really even to your parish or community or circle of friends, and you will have to forgive. This is perhaps one of the reasons why Christ did not emerge into human history as a full-grown man. He was born into a family so that He could experience what we experience, so that He could ask us to forgive those who trespass against us.

Prayer

Lord Jesus, Your family life was very private. We get a glimpse of it only here and there. For most of us family life is quite private too. Private joys and private hurts. Help us, Lord, to love and to learn from Your example. We also must sadly leave what we love. In a mysterious way You left Your family of eternal bliss, the holy Trinity, and came here for us. You understand. Amen.

CHRISTMAS SEASON
December 30

"She gave thanks to God and spoke about the Child to all who looked forward to the deliverance of Jerusalem" (Luke 2:38).

It is one of the blessings of religious history, in contrast to most other historical accounts, that it often tells us about the "little people." The vast majority of people at any time are on the sidelines. Their lives and even their deaths are directed by the very few who make the decisions that are recorded in world history. Thank God the Gospels are filled with little people. Anna, the focus of today's Gospel, is one of the first people we meet after the shepherds. Her walk through salvation history is a tender and revealing moment.

Anna, whose name means mercy or grace, was one of a known class of older widows who lived in the temple and served it both domestically and spiritually. I have seen such women with their tiny little bedrolls and few eating utensils living and working in the Buddhist temples of the Orient. They seemed largely unaware of the throngs of visitors and tourists; the temple was after all their home. They were so thin that they reminded me of the sparrows that one sometimes sees nesting inside great buildings.

Anna was eighty-four, an advanced age in those days, and never left the temple, spending her time in fasting and prayer. Being a prophetess, she, like Simeon, recognized that the baby was the one sent to deliver God's people. Also like Simeon, she saw with her eyes the salvation prepared by God.

We learn two things from Anna. The first is never to overlook the little people or to pass them by because they are not in the mainstream. Any intelligent person knows that the mainstream is usually going in the wrong direction and that the movers and shakers are almost always moving and shaking the wrong things. Recall Herod and Pilate. The really important people are those God counts as important.

The second thing to be learned from Anna is that we need to listen carefully to souls who are close to God. Recently a Cardinal archbishop with many years of education and experience told me that he learned most of the things he ever knew from holy old ladies. (Holy old men are more rare, but they are around.) Open your eyes. You may have been speaking to an Anna or a Simeon for years and never realized it.

Prayer

Holy Spirit, give me the grace to stop and listen to those who are close to You—far closer than I am. Help me to discern those who are old and wise and even now await our deliverance by the Son of God. Let me not be a fool like those who laughed at Anna and Simeon. Teach me to listen when You speak to me through those who, by grace and prayer, have received You with faith and love. Amen.

CHRISTMAS SEASON
December 31—Saint Sylvester, pope

"There is no one who has left house or brothers or sisters ... for my sake and for the gospel who will not receive a hundredfold now in this time ... with persecutions, and in the age to come eternal life"
(Mark 10:29-30).

Few people realize that on the last day of the year the Church commemorates the first pope after the terrible centuries of persecution by the Roman empire. Although he was not the very first bishop of Rome to die in bed, he surely grew up thinking he was going to be a martyr. As a boy he lived through the most ferocious persecution of all, that of Diocletian. Only a few years before he was elected pope in 314, the first decree of toleration of Christians was issued. One may suppose he made the same mistake we all make when times of terrible trial are over, that of thinking that things are finally going to work out and all will be peaceful with blue skies and roses.

Whatever Sylvester thought, he was in for stormy weather. Arianism, a heresy that ultimately denies the divinity of Christ, was spreading like wildfire. Sylvester's delegates would attend the first ecumenical council, which was held against Arius at Nicea in 325, and on his behalf they would approve its decrees. Also he had to put up with the Donatists, who, to use an old expression, were more Catholic than the pope and who taught that clergy who had buckled under persecution had lost their ordination. All was not dark, however. Following the Edict of Milan, which made Catholic Christianity the religion of the state, he presided over the exorcism of pagan temples and their consecration as churches. He also welcomed to Rome the first pilgrims to the tombs of the apostles Peter and Paul. There was as yet no Vatican art gallery, no collection of administrative offices, no diplomatic corps for him to oversee, but there was lots of trouble, and it was far from over when Saint Sylvester died.

Saint Sylvester's feast falls on New Year's Eve, when we happily bid the old year good-bye and wistfully hope that the next year will be better. For this reason each year the fourth-century pope always has a lesson for us: Keep going! Don't look back! Look ahead and trust God, but don't trust the next year will be wonderful. Rather be convinced that God will go with you. Christ will walk with anyone who invites him along. The Lord is my shepherd. Why should I be afraid? I don't expect everything to be wonderful next year; in fact, one of these years will be my last one on earth. I don't expect blue skies every day; that would mean a drought. But I do know that I will not be alone, because the lips of the man who was born in Bethlehem would say as he left this world thirty years later: "I will be with you always even to the end of the world" (Mt 28:20).

Prayer

Lord Jesus, as I end another year and prepare for the next one, make me ever more aware of Your presence. Help me to rest in Your presence even more than I have in the past. Help me spread the knowledge, the fragrance of Your presence wherever I go. Let more and more people know that You are with them, even in these anxious times. May this year, more than any previous one, be spent in Your presence. Amen.

CHRISTMAS SEASON
January 1 — Mary, Mother of God

"Why am I so favored that the mother of my Lord should come to me?" (Luke 1:43).

The Church in recent decades uses this day to call our attention to the Mother of Christ, who by the solemn decree of the Council of Ephesus (431) was declared to be the Mother of God, or God-bearer. Some have said that Mary is only the Mother of Jesus, and that God is Father of the Son. But the Child whom Mary conceived and bore in her womb was God. Jesus Christ is not two people, although He had both divine and human natures. The Child of Mary is a divine person, one who existed out of all eternity. She gave Him a human nature and a human body, as well as the occasion for the creation of His human soul. By her consent she freely gave Him the ability to suffer and die, which He did not have as God. Christ gave to Mary, and through her maternity to all of us, the ability to live forever with Him.

The figure of the chaste and loving Madonna has been a favorite one in Christian art and song. Her intercession and prayer are sought beyond those of all other saints in heaven. Her mysterious privileges are celebrated by the Church in both East and West. All this fulfills her own words: "All generations shall call me blessed" (Lk 1:48).

For the individual Christian the fact that Mary, a human being, is the Mother of the Son of God is the clearest possible link between the human and the divine. Christ came from above; Mary came from below, from our own human stock, the people of the earth. Human means from the earth, and humility means bent low to the earth. Mary has both these qualities, and they often do not go together. Our Advent meditations did not include her Immaculate Conception, that is, a total freedom from the effects of original sin, a unique favor God granted in order to prepare her to be the Mother of His Son. Even the Protestant reformers who rejected the idea of praying for Mary's intercession admitted their belief that she was always free from sin—the one who is "full of grace."

Try to spend a little time today in the light of Mary's gifts and blessings. They come from God, and they lead entirely to her Son. But these gifts have their own important message. Our poor broken human nature has one perfect reflection: a little peasant girl—the original Cinderella—who has became the Mother of the children of God.

Prayer

Lord Jesus Christ, You are like us because You had a mother. Though pure and holy, she, like You, experienced life as we do, but without sin. You suffered, she suffered, we suffer. You enjoyed the little things of life. She did too, and so do we. Help us always to be faithful, as Your Mother was. May her words be our meditation every day: "Be it done unto me according to thy word" (Lk 1:38). Amen.

CHRISTMAS SEASON
January 2—Saints Basil the Great and Gregory Nazianzen

"He is the source of your life in Christ Jesus, whom God made our wisdom, our righteousness and sanctification and redemption" (1 Cor 1:30).

When the Word of God came into the world, He came through the Holy Spirit, and then He sent the Holy Spirit to all who believe in Him. The Spirit of God gives many gifts to anyone who is willing to receive them. The most precious of all is wisdom. We don't think of wisdom very often in our culture. We don't value wise people. In fact, this adjective is often used in a sarcastic way, as in the expression, "He's a wise guy." Most Christians pay lip service to wisdom, often not even knowing what it is.

Christ gives wisdom because He is the wisdom of God. He is not simply wise; He embodies wisdom, as well as goodness, justice, truth, and beauty. If we recognize His gift of wisdom, it is because He has helped us to do so. Very simply, wisdom leads us to put things in order, to organize our priorities rightly. Every element of our lives can be ordered by wisdom. It teaches us the proper measure of less important things so that they serve, and do not contradict, the greater gifts of God. The apex of wisdom is to "seek first the kingdom of God and his righteousness, and all these things will be added unto you" (Mt 6:33). This takes a great deal of honest thought and even courage. For example, if we need a car, do we waste money foolishly on an expensive car?

Or do we buy only what we need and then use any extra money to help others on their way to God? This is really a radical thought. When we take recreation, is it simple and focused, and does it include time for quiet reflection and prayer? Or do we waste time and resources, so that often there is no gain to our Christian life at all? In the process of wasting our resources, do we help corrupt the lives of others?

It is wisdom to avoid vanity, to organize one's life even in its tiresome and painful parts around the kingdom of God. A wise person can use even a terminal illness to grow in the kingdom of God, and a fool can ruin his health abusing things in a way that goes against the teachings of Jesus, who is Truth itself.

Today the Church honors two men from the East who lived in the fourth century, Saint Basil, father of Eastern monasticism, and Saint Gregory, a pioneering theologian. Their lives were filled with challenges, misunderstandings, and even failures. But these two close friends, both bishops, kept their eyes on the teachings of Jesus and their hearts open to His wisdom.

When Basil died, Gregory preached a great sermon to the huge assembled crowd. He said that we must not weep but rejoice, because Basil was already in heaven praying for us and joining in the heavenly sacrifice. In this way he affirmed the reality of eternal life in Christ and even the permanence of the priesthood.

Prayer

Lord Jesus Christ, send Your Holy Spirit's gift of wisdom into my life and into the lives of those I love. Help us each day to sort things out wisely, to ignore what is meaningless, and to seek the good of others, especially through things that bring them closer to You. Awaken in us a strong desire for Your gifts, which alone do not pass away. Amen.

CHRISTMAS SEASON
January 3 (Christmas weekday)

"Those who are led by the Spirit of God are the children of God" (Romans 8:14).

Thousands of times we have repeated the phrase "Our Father." But how are we actually His children? The simple answer is, As often as we do the works of God and follow His commandments and the teachings of His Son. It is not enough to be united with Christ by faith. Saint James reminds us that even the devils believe and tremble before Him (see Jas 2:14ff). And it is certainly not enough simply to do good works prescribed by the Gospel. It is necessary to be open as much as we can to the life of Christ in our own being. This means that in our own circumstances we must do what He did and act as He acted and even think His thoughts. "Let that mind be in you which was in Christ Jesus" (Phil 2:5). This is a very big job, the work of a lifetime, and for several reasons one must not get discouraged.

The first is that our union with Christ does not depend on our own doing. It is God's gift of life to our spirit, just as our flesh is also His gift. But this gift is much higher because the flesh perishes while the spirit has everlasting life. We can go through this day growing in the life of Christ, insofar as we want to, by accepting His grace. This is not an abstract idea, and it's not vague at all.

During the day several incidents will occur in which we can choose to act in a Christian way. They may be small, like a gesture of courtesy or friendliness to a stranger. They may be opportunities for charity completely unnoticed by others. They may involve something more difficult, like forgiveness or not striking back when offended. We may be offered the opportunity to reject temptation or bear witness to the truth when it is unpopular. We may be asked to do the right thing when there are serious consequences, like losing a job or the help that we ourselves needed desperately. All these incidents I have described are given in the Sermon on the Mount. If these opportunities to follow Jesus Christ are ignored, then Christianity is hollow. The Lord knows that we do not even see the immense number of opportunities we have to follow Christ, because we do not have the right mind-set. We must have that mind which was in Christ Jesus.

As the Christmas season draws to a close, we have a great chance to make our lives a bit different as a result of the commemoration of Christ's birth. Listen to the voice of the Spirit in your heart in quiet meditation over the Scriptures. "The Spirit himself bears witness to our spirit that we are children of God, and if children, then heirs, heirs of God and joint heirs with Christ, if only we suffer with him that we may be glorified with him" (Rom 8:15–17).

Prayer

Jesus, my Master, give me the grace to follow You each day more faithfully. May Your Holy Spirit point out the occasions and help me to do things in a different way so as to follow You more faithfully. You are our only true and lasting light. May my life be a faint reflection for those around me who are struggling to see the way. Amen.

CHRISTMAS SEASON
January 4 — Saint Elizabeth Seton

"Praise to the holy woman whose home is built on faithful love and whose pathway leads to God"
(Entrance antiphon for Mass).

During the week of the Epiphany, when we celebrate Christ's manifestation to the Gentiles who are represented by the Magi, or wise men, Catholics in America commemorate three saints of their own. Each one uniquely represents the Christian life as it may be lived in modern times and in a very real way. The passage of centuries has not made the lives of these great Christians static or remote, like stained-glass windows of Saint Francis or Saint Teresa. We are so much closer in time to these three saints from North America that we have a more realistic picture of them. They lived in the real world that we know. All of them used steam travel, and one even used an automobile. So often time removes some of the realism of the saints of the past.

Saint Elizabeth Seton was a convert, mother, widow, and founder of a religious community, the Sisters of Charity. She raised five children and cared for most of them, as she had for her husband, when they were dying of tuberculosis. She was born into a prominent Episcopalian family in New York in 1774. Following her husband's death, she was drawn to enter the then despised Catholic Church when she was thirty-one, having been greatly impressed by the devotion to the presence of Christ in the Eucharist she had observed in Italy.

In line with our thinking about how to be a real Christian, it must be said of this intrepid woman that she rarely missed a chance to do so. Her life is a litany of opportunities to follow Christ and his Gospel with unflinching determination—teaching, serving the poor, preparing her beloved children for death without complaints. If you are reading this meditation, Saint Elizabeth has some suggestions for you. Never say no when you can say yes to an opportunity to serve God and his children. Think about that. And when disasters occur, don't feel resentful and ill-used and complain that they shouldn't happen to you because you are a faithful Christian. Elizabeth felt her mother's heart break as apprehension turned to the terrible certainty that one after another of her children did not just have a cold but that they would cough themselves into the grave as her husband had. She did not complain. She did not ask why. Instead she asked, "What should I do?"

As one of the millions of Americans who learned about the Christian life from the Sisters and Daughters of Charity, I can only pray that the spirit of these great Christian women religious who taught me in several different communities will return to its former strength. Sure, some of the sisters did not achieve the highest spiritual goals; some were crabby, and some were a bit twisted. But after fifty years I am moved to tears when I think of a number of great intrepid sisters I have known.

Saint Elizabeth translated *A Treatise on Interior Peace* by Father Ambroise de Lombez, an eighteenth-century French Capuchin writer. The following line from her translation is a practical thought for any day on your journey. "The love of God produces submission of our will to all the orders of his providence; and our submission preserves us in a holy tranquility amidst the most painful reverses, and an admirable equilibrium of mind through the greatest agitations and most cruel vicissitudes of life." [4]

Prayer

Lord Jesus, give me a strong and firm faith even in the face of adversity or tragedy. Let me not be deterred by the recognition that I must carry the crosses that everyone else carries, even unbelievers. Help me to know that the difference comes from the faith in which we do these things and the love with which we accept them. Amen.

CHRISTMAS SEASON
January 5 — Saint John Neumann

"I will give you shepherds after my own heart, who will feed you with knowledge and understanding"
(Jeremiah 3:15).

John Neumann was one of millions of nineteenth-century immigrants who came to the New World with a few bits of clothing and some articles, most religious, packed in a sack. At Ellis Island a touching display of religious articles—Jewish prayer shawls, Protestant Bibles, icons and statues of Jesus and Mary—remind us that almost all these immigrants brought with them a strong faith in God from their homeland. The ancestors of most people reading this book are among them. John Neumann came from Bohemia, hoping to work as a priest, and was ordained by the bishop of New York in 1836. To further his goal to be a missionary and to grow in the Christian life, he joined the Redemptorist Order, which had been founded by Saint Alphonsus a century before to do exactly this.

After years of hard work and very much aware of his own limitations, he was made bishop of Philadelphia, which he saw as a city of such elegance and sophistication that he felt the work was beyond his competence. Fortunately, his humility was matched by his trust in God and his willingness to carry the cross. In his eight short years as bishop he opened almost fifty parishes, many schools, founded a community of teaching sisters, and began the building of the cathedral.

Anyone reading Bishop Neumann's life realizes that his humility was entwined with what we now call a negative self-image and that he suffered from the same neurosis that most responsible people are familiar with. He also experienced a dose of natural melancholy, or depression. But—and this is the really important message of this great Christian—it never got him down. In fact, it never stood in the way at all. In our age, which has spirituality mixed up with forms of mental health often sounding like disguised forms of narcissism or self-love, people easily get confused. And while one must not feed a neurosis and may need a bit of counseling to keep it from getting out of hand, the Gospel way is the way for everyone, neurotic or not. It is the way given by the Way. Christ says "Follow Me" to everyone. John Neumann was a man of immense charity, energy, and concern for others. In his own words he asked the Vatican to let him leave Philadelphia and work on the farms, in the mines and forests, with humble and struggling folk, among whom he would feel most at home. In fact, he was on an errand of mercy when God called his servant home.

The message of Christmas is to imitate God and His Son in their absolute self-giving. To become a better Christian is to be drawn more and more into this torrent of love. Many neurotic souls have stopped worrying about themselves and imitated Christ in his generosity. As a priest and bishop, John Neumann gave himself completely for his faith. He explicitly felt a responsibility to help as best he could every living soul in his diocese whether they were of his own faith or of no faith. Saint Augustine says that the best religion is to imitate what you worship. In the life of this very humble immigrant, a man of intense prayer, we see a call to imitate the Christ we adore.

Prayer

Lord Jesus, give me Your Spirit that I may follow Your generosity and thoughtfulness. Take away my hurts, my stupidly cherished wounds, my fears. Help me find my joy in serving You and all members of Your flock, remembering that we are all Your sheep and all shepherds to one another. Amen.

CHRISTMAS SEASON
January 6 — Blessed André Bessette

"May all your works praise you, Lord, and your saints bless you. They will tell the glory of your kingdom and proclaim your power"
(Psalm 145:10).

In all the solemnity of this time we must be careful not to overlook one of America's remarkable and endearing characters, a little Canadian farmer boy who in the most unlikely way would become the saint of Montreal. Brother André is such a man of our times that as a child I remember all the excitement when he came to Jersey City and did not realize that the crowds were there to see him. A lay brother (not a teaching brother) of the Holy Cross Congregation, he was assigned to be the doorkeeper at their college at the foot of Mount Royal. He had a great devotion to Saint Joseph, another humble man who was known only for his loving care of the Son of God. Brother André wanted to build a shrine church and got a modest one going. I suspect that many more sensible people considered it all a pious nothing. But André was a friend of God and one of those rare souls such as we meet in the Bible. The Lord heard his prayers in marvelous ways. The sick were cured, the lost returned to God, and troubled families were healed. In honor of His humble foster father, the Son of God would show forth His power to those who came to Brother André with simple faith. The little shrine became a huge impressive basilica visible for miles away from Mount Royal.

In the very first centuries Christ the Healer had been the focus of a beautiful devotion. Brother André became one of many saints who through the ages have been known as miracle workers. These people with a vocation to be eaten alive by crowds of suffering people found that the gift of healing was itself a great cross. But André, like other saintly heroes, kept right on going, unfatigued and undaunted and unswerving in His call to honor the humble carpenter whom God Himself had chosen to be the head of his house.

The Magi probably paid little attention to Joseph. He stood on the side, performing His tasks—works of love for His wife and her mysterious child. But the angel of the Lord spoke to Joseph to save the child from Herod. Joseph did what he was told and was given the improbable command to go through the dangerous desert to Egypt. Brother André also built his shrine very improbably. We have a lot to learn from these two men brought together by devotion to Christ and his Mother. We have to learn to listen to God's Word and to do what we are told.

Prayer

Lord Jesus Christ, how well You knew Joseph, and how mysterious it is for him to love You as his own son. Providence has told us little about this man, and so we hardly notice him. He is like the Magi. But Lord, we ask to be a little part in the great drama of salvation, for we can be saved only if we have a part with You. Amen.

CHRISTMAS SEASON
The Epiphany of the Lord
(Sunday following January 1)

"When they saw the star, they rejoiced exceedingly with great joy; and on entering the house, they found the Child with Mary his Mother, and they fell down and worshipped him" (Matthew 2:10-11).

Today Christians celebrate a marvelous theophany of our religion: the showing of the Messiah to the Gentiles. Theophanies are very important events in the history of salvation, but because of the skepticism of our time, which can even intimidate Christian scholars, they are played down with a patronizing smile. Candidly, this makes me sick. Why? A theophany is a manifestation of God's power and presence, which is perceived by all who are present. It is the supernatural occurring in the natural world for all to see. Scripture abounds with them, and several are key events in salvation history, for example, the burning bush, and the Exodus from Egypt with the leading cloud and pillar of fire. Apart from the star of Bethlehem, there are other theophanies which the Church celebrates today: turning the water into wine at Cana, and the divine voice and the appearance of the dovelike figure at the baptism of Christ. The Resurrection, including the risen body of Christ, is also a theophany.

At least one theophany occurred in the twentieth century when thousands of people, whether believers or nonbelievers, observed what appeared to be a whirling sun changing colors and coming close to the earth. This occurred at Fatima, Portugal, on October 13, 1917.

Anticlerical newspapers carried the reports of this theophany, written by unbelieving professors of science at the state university in Lisbon.

Some—even believers—will dismiss the account of the star and the Magi as a myth or a parable. A mere story. But they were not there. The basis of their rejection is not the improbability of the occurrence, which is certainly no more improbable than the birth of the Messiah itself. The real basis of their skepticism is a failure to accept any mystery, even those of science. They reject the supernatural, and yet no one has a definition of matter or even a comprehension of what is light or time or life.

Through the Holy Spirit, Divine Providence has given to the Church these and many other mysterious accounts of supernatural occurrences to guide us in our faith. Billions of Christians have rejoiced in the star and this proclamation of the King of Kings. As a man, this Child would speak to the wind and the sea, and they would obey Him. He would turn water into wine, multiply loaves and fish, and call the dead back to life. Because of the Holy Spirit's gift known as revelation, I believe it. I was not there. Some do not believe it, but they were not there either. They must believe in their unbelief, because they cannot prove that it did not happen.

Christian friend, take your choice. Mysteries abound in revelation. To quibble about them is what Christ calls little faith, a dark turning toward unbelief, which leads nowhere but to oblivion. Every clear night of the year I look up to the stars. I recall the Gospels, and I believe. I regret only that I do not believe enough to follow the star King more faithfully.

Prayer

Jesus, true Light, shine in the darkness of my soul. Increase my faith, dispel doubt, guide my thoughts to keep faith alive in the darkest night. Your light will come again, and all will see the salvation from our God. Amen.

CHRISTMAS SEASON
The Baptism of the Lord
(Sunday following Epiphany)

"This is my beloved Son with whom
I am well pleased" (Matthew 3:17).
"The crowd standing by heard it and said that
it had thundered. Others said, 'An angel has
spoken to him'" (John 12:29).

The Church celebrates several theophanies in the life of Christ. The manifestation of God and the approbation of His Son, made through the voice of the Father, took place at the Lord's baptism. This mysterious event is very important because the Father proclaims Jesus' divinity at the very moment when His Son is acting like a repentant sinner. Baptism is actually a sign of repentance, of cleansing by God, in several world religions. Jesus is baptized to give us good example and perhaps as a sign that He has taken on Himself the sins of us all. As with the Epiphany, some see this account as another story to enhance belief in the divinity of Christ. Some claim that it is merely a myth. When a similar event is recorded (see Jn 12:27-30) and Jesus hears the Father's voice, some of the bystanders claimed that it had thundered. This explanation reminds me of flimsy mind games of people who cannot accept miracles. Caught in a misunderstanding of the nature of physical science, they simply repeat the old refrain: It cannot be. The pope has been very critical of this kind of thinking. He calls it a rationalist "prejudice against the supernatural."[5] But let's move on to see beyond these scholars and their timid thoughts.

Jesus of Nazareth, as we have seen, is a divine person who took to Himself a true human body and a human soul. He also had a human will. This interpretation was accepted by the early Church on the basis of His words in Gethsemane, "Father ... not my will but thy will be done" (Lk 22:42). If Jesus' will had been simply the divine will, the thought of our imitating Him would be somewhat pointless. We can be imitators of God in some ways, through generosity and forgiveness, but certainly not in others. We cannot imitate Christ when His divine power is operating. We cannot command the waves of the sea or call back the dead from their graves.

But we can imitate Him in His blessed humanity. He goes on when He is tired; He labors on with effort when He is fatigued. He is kind and generous and understanding. He goes to dinner at the houses of less respectable people and defends them against the self-righteous. At His baptism his two natures come together in a single experience of humility. Both His divinity and His humanity are involved. The Father, who can be seen in every aspect of the life He chooses for His Son—poverty, misunderstanding, vulnerability to abuse—this same Father announces His pleasure at his Son's act of humility in submitting to John's baptism. John the Baptist was perfectly logical in not wanting to baptize the one he called the Lamb of God who takes away the sins of the world (see Jn 1:29). But Jesus follows the highest wisdom, the wisdom of the Father. We must silently adore this wise humility.

Prayer

O Lord Jesus Christ, help me to be Your disciple. Give me Your grace that I may want to follow You and grant me the ability to do so. Require of me what You will and give me the grace and help to do it. Along with those I love, may I come closer to You, with whom the Father is well pleased. Amen.

A Final Thought

During these meditations we have focused on what we can learn by faithfully reflecting on the coming of the Son. We draw these to a close with our Lord's baptism. There is no end to what we can learn from the Incarnate Word of God, from Jesus of Nazareth. Stay close to His Word and to the ancient interpretation of that Word, which is the foundation of the Christian faith. The ancient Fathers would coin new words not in the Gospel: Trinity, Incarnation, Redemption, and many others to try to maintain the faith as the Teacher of God inspired the thinking of men. Guided by the Holy Spirit, the Fathers have passed the Scriptures and the traditional interpretation of them to us. From their point of view, the Gospel is one long act of dedication to our Savior.

111

Prayer

O Lord Jesus Christ, my Savior, who as eternal Son of God humbly came into this world, help my unbelief. May I grow in an ever richer and stronger faith in the mystery of Your Incarnation and the salvation that it brought. Free me from the skepticism and timidity of our times.

Send Your Holy Spirit on our world, on all those I know and care about. Give them a new and stronger faith. Ask Your heavenly Father, who has sent You, to draw them so that they may believe in You.

Accompany each one of us as the Good Shepherd and protect us from error, confusion, and unbelief. And help us to live our faith. If we indeed believe that You came as our brother into this world, then we must accept your teachings and live according to them. We must love our neighbor as ourselves. We must reach out as You told us to in the parable of the Good Samaritan. We must teach more by what we do than by what we say. And may the example of a Christian life, even a moment of that life, be the cause of a growing faith in those who seem so lost in the darkness of unbelief.

Jesus, Good Shepherd of our souls, You came to save the world. We ask You to save it. You died for each individual soul. Implore Your heavenly Father so that He may draw each of us closer to You. Grant that as we live through the events of Your life each year, symbolically presented, we may experience more fully Your great love for us in becoming a human being. And may we return that love always with gratitude and awe. We pray to You, Christ our Lord. Amen.

Part Two

HYMNS, PRAYERS, AND SPIRITUAL READINGS

On the Mystery of the Incarnation

A meditative prayer, such as this one by John Henry Newman (1801–1890), is a good way to compose our mind and spirit and elevate our heart at the beginning of any period of prayer or reflective reading.

A Short Visit With Christ in the Blessed Sacrament
Before Meditation

I place myself in the presence of Him, in whose Incarnate Presence I am before I place myself there.

I adore Thee, O my Savior, present here as God and man, in soul and body, in true flesh and blood.

I acknowledge and confess that I kneel before that Sacred Humanity, which was conceived in Mary's womb, and lay in Mary's bosom; which grew up to man's estate, and by the Sea of Galilee called the Twelve, wrought miracles, and spoke words of wisdom and peace; which in due season hung on the cross, lay in the tomb, rose from the dead, and now reigns in heaven.

I praise, and bless, and give myself wholly to Him, who is the true Bread of my soul, and my everlasting joy.

───

The following hymns are suitable for meditation or even singing during the holy seasons of Advent and Christmas. We have included works of beauty and insight that are not readily available in standard parish hymnals.

Hark! A Mystic Voice Is Sounding

*There have been many translations of this fifth- to sixth-century Ambrosian-style hymn, **En clara vox redarguit**, which has often been used at Lauds during Advent. This one is by Father Edward Caswall.*

Hark! a mystic voice is sounding,
"Christ is nigh," it seems to say,
"Cast away the dreams of darkness,
O ye children of the day."

Startled at the solemn warning,
Let the earthbound soul arise;
Christ, her Sun, all sloth dispelling,
Shines upon the morning skies.

Lo! the Lamb so long expected,
Comes with pardon down from Heav'n,
Let us haste, with tears of sorrow,
One and all to be forgiv'n.

So when next He comes with glory,
Wrapping all the earth in fear,
May He then as our Defender,
On the clouds of Heav'n appear.

Honor, glory, virtue, merit
To the Father and the Son,
With the co-eternal Spirit,
While eternal ages run.

Behold! Behold He Cometh

This hymn, also suitable for Advent, was translated from the Latin by Claudia Hernaman (1838–98) and set to music by Samuel Webbe (1740–1816).

Behold! behold He cometh,
Who doth salvation bring;
Lift up your hands rejoicing,
And welcome Zion's King;
With hymns of joy we praise the Lord,
Hosanna to th'Incarnate Word!

Hosanna to the Saviour,
Who came on Christmas morn,
And of a lowly Virgin,
Was in a stable born;
Emmanuel! Dear Jesus, come,
Within Thy children make Thy home!

Yea, come in love and meekness,
Our Saviour now to be;
Come to be formed in us,
And make us like to Thee,
Before the day of wrath draw near,
When as our Judge Thou shalt appear.

Soon shalt Thou sit in glory
Upon the great white Throne,
And punish all the wicked,
And recompense Thine own;
When ev'ry word and deed and thought
To righteous judgment shall be brought.

Conditor Alme Siderum

This seventh-century Ambrosian composition, also known as **Creator Alme Siderum**, *is a traditional Advent Vespers hymn containing references both to Christ's first coming at his Nativity and his second coming at the end of the world.*

Bright builder of the heavenly poles,
Eternal light of faithful souls,
Jesus, Redeemer of mankind,
Our humble prayers vouchsafe to mind.

Who, lest the fraud of hell's black king
Should all men to destruction bring,
Didst, by an act of generous love,
The fainting world's physician prove.

Thou, that Thou mightst our ransom pay
And wash the stains of sin away,
Didst from a Virgin's womb proceed
And on the Cross a victim bleed.

Thy glorious power, Thy saving name
No sooner any voice can frame,
But heaven and earth and hell agree
To honor them with trembling knee.

Thee, Christ, who at the latter day
Shalt be our Judge, we humbly pray
Such arms of heavenly grace to send
As may Thy Church from foes defend.

Be glory given and honor done
To God the Father and the Son
And to the Holy Ghost on high,
From age to age eternally.

See, Amid the Winter's Snow

*Father Edward Caswall (1814–78), mentioned above as translator, is the author of this hymn. A companion to Newman at the Birmingham Oratory, he was similarly a convert and former Anglican priest. He published a series of breviary hymns as **Lyra Catholica** in 1849.*

See, amid the winter's snow,
Born for us on earth below;
See the tender lamb appears,
Promised from eternal years!

Refrain: Hail, thou ever blessed morn,
Hail, Redemption's happy dawn!
Sing through all Jerusalem,
Christ is born in Bethlehem.

Lo, within a manger lies
He who built the starry skies;
He, who throned in heights sublime,
Sits amid the Cherubim. (Refrain)

Sacred Infant all divine,
What a tender love was Thine;
Thus to come from highest bliss,
Down to such a world as this. (Refrain)

Teach, oh teach us, holy Child,
By Thy Face so meek and mild;
Teach us to resemble Thee
In Thy sweet humility. (Refrain)

Virgin Mother, Mary blest
By the joys that fill thy breast,
Pray for us, that we may prove
Worthy of the Saviour's love. (Refrain)

⚬⚬⚬

Four traditional English-language Christmas carols follow:

The Snow Lay On The Ground

A West of England carol, here rendered by the well-known historian, the Rev. Dr. John Lingard (1771–1851).

The snow lay on the ground,
The stars shone bright,
When Christ our Lord was born
On Christmas night.

'Twas Mary, daughter pure
Of holy Anne,
That brought into this world,
The God made Man.

She laid Him in a stall
At Bethlehem;
The ass, and oxen shared
The roof with them.

Saint Joseph too was by,
To tend the Child;
To guard Him, and protect
His Mother mild.

The angels hovered round,
And sang this song;
"Venite, adore-
mus Dominum."

And then that manger poor
Became a throne;
For He whom Mary bore
Was God the Son.

O come, then, let us join
The heav'nly host,
To praise the Father, Son
And Holy Ghost.

A Hereford Carol

One of the many English regional carols of medieval origin.

Come, all you faithful Christians
That dwell here on earth,
Come, celebrate the morning
Of our dear Saviour's birth.
This is the happy morning,
This is the blessèd morn:
To save our souls from ruin,
The Son of God was born.

Behold the angel Gabriel,
In Scripture it is said,
Did with his holy message
Come to the virgin maid:
"Hail, blest among all women!"
He thus did greet her then,
"Lo, thou shalt be the mother
Of the Saviour of all men."

Her time being accomplished,
She came to Bethlehem,
And then was safe delivered
Of the Saviour of all men.
No princely pomp attended Him,
His honors were but small;
A manger was His cradle,
His bed an ox's stall.

Now to Him that is ascended
Let all our praises be;
May we His steps then follow,
And He our pattern be;
So when our lives are ended,
We all may hear Him call:
"Come, souls, receive the kingdom,
Preparèd for you all."

A Virgin Most Pure, As the Prophets Did Tell

An ancient carol. The author's identity is lost in time.

A Virgin most pure, as the prophets did tell,
Hath brought forth a Savior, as it hath befell,
To be our Redeemer from death, hell and sin,
Which Adam's transgression had wrapped us in.

Refrain: Rejoice and be merry,
                    Set sorrow aside,
                    Christ Jesus our Savior
                    Was born on this tide.

In Bethlehem city in Jewry it was,
Where Joseph and Mary together did pass,
And there to be taxed with many one mo',
For Caesar commanded the same should be so. (Refrain)

But when they had entered the city so fair,
A number of people so mighty was there
That Mary and Joseph, whose substance was small,
Could procure in the Inn no lodging at all. (Refrain)

Then they were constrained in a stable to lie,
Where oxen and asses they used there to tie;
Their lodging so simple they held it no scorn,
But against the next morning a Savior was born. (Refrain)

The King of glory to this world being brought,
Small store of fine linen to wrap Him was sought;
When Mary had swaddled her young Son so sweet,
Within an ox manger she laid Him to sleep. (Refrain)

Then God sent an angel from heaven so high
To certain poor shepherds in fields where they lie,
And charged them no longer in sorrow to stay,
Because that our Savior was born on this day. (Refrain)

Then presently after the shepherds did spy
A number of angels appear in the sky;
Who joyfully talked and sweetly did sing,
"To God be all glory, our heavenly King." (Refrain)

An Irish Carol

Like many Christmas carols, this one grew out of folk melodies of perhaps the sixteenth or seventeenth century.

Christmas Day is come; let's all prepare for mirth,
Which fills the heavens and earth at this amazing birth.
Through both the joyous angels in strife and hurry fly,
With glory and hosannas, "All Holy" do they cry,
In heaven the Church triumphant adores with all her choirs,
The militant on earth with humble faith admires.

But why should we rejoice? Should we not rather mourn
To see the hope of nations thus in a stable born?
Where are His crown and sceptre, where is His throne
    sublime,
Where is His train majestic that should the stars outshine?
Is there no sumptuous palace nor any inn at all
To lodge His heavenly mother but in a filthy stall?

Oh! cease, ye blessed angels, such clamorous joys to make!
Though midnight silence favors, the shepherds are awake;
And you, O glorious star! that with new splendor brings
From the remotest parts three learned eastern kings,
Turn somewhere else your lustre, your rays elsewhere
    display;
For Herod he may slay the Babe, and Christ must straight
    away.

If we would then rejoice, let's cancel the old score,
And, purposing amendment, resolve to sin no more,
For mirth can ne'er content us, without a conscience clear;
And thus we'll find true pleasure in all the usual cheer,
In dancing, sporting, revelling, with masquerade and drum,
So let our Christmas merry be, as Christmas doth become.

Hark! The Herald Host Is Singing

This Christmas hymn was set to music by the German composer Engelbert Humperdinck (1854–1921).

Hark! The herald host is singing,
Thro' the silent holy night,
Tidings of great joy they're bringing,
From yon starry azure height.
And each heart is filled with gladness,
At the message which they bring:
"Christ is born, forget all sadness,
Trust in Him, your Savior King."

And behold the stars bright glowing,
Shed o'er earth their radiant light,
While from Angels' lips are flowing
Anthems thro' the holy night.
Bright each window now is glowing,
Lighted by the Christmas tree;
And each cheek with joy is glowing,
And each heart is filled with glee.

Soft the messengers from Heaven
Wing their flight from home to home:
Bearing lessons God hath given
Unto all on earth that roam.
"Welcome, welcome Christmas evening
Bringing peace and love to earth!"
Show your gratitude, rejoicing,
Christians in your Savior's birth!

The following two hymns have been popular in modern times,
both in liturgical and nonliturgical settings.

When Blossoms Flowered 'Mid the Snows
(Gesù Bambino)

*Italian-born composer Pietro A. Yon (1886–1943), who was organist at
St. Patrick's Cathedral, New York, in the 1930s, is known for his many
compositions of church music. This translation is by the American librettist Frederick H. Martens (1874–1932).*

When blossoms flowered 'mid the snows
Upon a winter night,
Was born the Child, the Christmas Rose,
The King of Love and Light.
The angels sang, the shepherds sang,
The grateful earth rejoiced;
And at His blessed birth the stars
Their exultation voiced.

O come let us adore Him,
O come let us adore Him,
O come let us adore Him,
Christ the Lord.

When gain the heart with rapture glows
To greet the holy night,
That gave the world its Christmas Rose,
Its King of Love and Light.
Let ev'ry voice acclaim His name,
The grateful chorus swell.

From paradise to earth He came
That we with Him might dwell.

O come let us adore Him,
O come let us adore Him,
O come let us adore Him,
Christ the Lord.

O Holy Night
(Cantique de Noël)

Paris-born Adolphe Adam (1803–56) is the composer of this Christmas hymn, translated here by the American musician and critic J.S. Dwight (1813–93).

O holy night the stars are brightly shining,
It is the night of the dear Savior's birth;
Long lay the world in sin and sorrow pining,
Till He appeared and the soul felt its worth.
A thrill of hope the weary world rejoices,
For yonder breaks a new and glorious morn!
Fall on your knees! O hear the angel voices
O night divine! O night when Christ was born!
O night divine! O night, O night divine!

Led by the light of faith serenely beaming,
With glowing heart by His cradle we stand;
So led by light of a star sweetly gleaming,
Here came the Wise Men from the Orient land.
The King of kings lay thus in lowly manger,
In all our trials born to be our Friend;

He knows our need, He guardeth us from danger,
Behold your King! before the Lowly bend!
Behold your King! before the Lowly bend!

Truly He taught us to love one another;
His law is Love and His Gospel is peace;
Chains shall He break, for the slave is our brother,
And in His name, all oppression shall cease.
With hymns of joy in grateful chorus raising,
Let every heart adore His holy name!
Christ is the Lord! With saint and seraph praising,
His pow'r and glory evermore proclaim!
His pow'r and glory evermore proclaim!

Jesu, Redemptor Omnium

This Vespers hymn for Christmas Day dates from the sixth century.

Jesus! Redeemer of the world!
Who, ere the earliest dawn of light,
Wast from eternal ages born,
Immense in glory as in might.

Immortal hope of all mankind
In whom the Father's face we see,
Hear Thou the prayers Thy people pour
This day throughout the world to Thee.

Remember, O Creator Lord!
That in the Virgin's sacred womb
Thou wast conceiv'd and of her flesh
Didst our mortality assume.

This ever blest recurring day
Its witness bears, that all alone,
From Thy own Father's bosom forth,
To save the world Thou camest down.

O Day! To which the seas and sky,
And earth, and heav'n, glad welcome sing;
O Day! which heal'd our misery,
And brought on earth salvation's King.

We, too, O Lord, who have been cleans'd
In Thy own fount of Blood divine,
Offer the tribute of sweet song
On this blest natal day of Thine.

O Jesu! born of Virgin bright,
Immortal glory be to Thee;
Praise to the Father infinite
And Holy Ghost eternally. Amen.

Salvete, flores martyrum

Sung at Vespers on the feast of the Holy Innocents, this hymn was composed by the poet Prudentius (348–413).

Flowers of martyrdom, all hail!
Smitten by the tyrant foe
On life's threshold, as the gale
Strews the roses ere they blow.

First to bleed for Christ, sweet Lambs!
What a simple death ye died!
Playing with your wreaths and palms,
At the very altar side.

Honor, glory, virtue, merit
Be to Thee, O Virgin's Son!
With the Father, and the Spirit
While eternal ages run. Amen.

Jesu Dulcis Memoria

Long thought to be the work of Saint Bernard, this beautiful late-twelfth-century hymn was traditionally sung at Vespers on the feast of the Holy Name of Jesus. We give Father Caswall's translation.

Jesu, the very thought of Thee
With sweetness fills my breast,
But sweeter far Thy face to see
And in Thy presence rest.

Nor voice can sing, nor heart can frame,
Nor can the memory find,
A sweeter sound than Thy blest Name,
O Savior of mankind.

O hope of every contrite heart,
O joy of all the meek,
To those who fall, how kind Thou art!
How good to those who seek.

But what to those who find? Ah! this
Nor tongue nor pen can show;
The love of Jesus, what it is,
None but His loved ones know.

Jesu, our only joy be Thou,
As Thou our prize wilt be,
Jesu, be Thou our glory now,
And through eternity.   Amen.

Crudelis Herodes

This Vespers hymn for the feast of the Epiphany is attributed to the fifth-century Roman poet Sedulius. It contains allusions to the triple theophanies linked with this feast. (See mediation for Epiphany day.)

O cruel Herod! why thus fear thy King and God,
Who comes below?
No earthly crown comes He to take,
Who heavenly kingdoms doth bestow.

The wise Magi see the star
And follow as it leads before;
By its pure ray they seek the light,
And with their gifts that Light adore.

Behold at length the heavenly Lamb
Baptiz'd in Jordan's sacred flood;
There consecrating by His touch
Water to cleanse us in His blood.

But Cana saw her glorious Lord
Begin His miracles divine;
When water reddening at His word,
Flow'd forth obedient as wine.

To Thee, O Jesu, who Thyself
Hast to the Gentile world displayed,
Praise, with the Father evermore,
And with the Holy Ghost, be paid. Amen.

O Lux Beata Caelitum

This Vespers hymn for the feast of the Holy Family was written by Pope Leo XIII (1810–1903).

O highest hope of mortals,
Blest light of saints above,
O Jesus, on whose boyhood
Home smiled with kindly love.

O Thou whose bosom nursed Him,
O Mary highly graced,
Whose breast gave milk to Jesus,
Whose arms thy God embraced;

And thou of all men chosen
To guard the Virgin's fame,
To whom God's Son refused not
A father's gracious name;

Born for the nation's healing
Of Jesse's lineage high,
Behold the suppliants kneeling,
O hear the sinner's cry.

The sun, returned to evening,
Dusks all the twilight air;
We, lingering here before you,
Pour out our heartfelt prayer.

Your home was a garden,
Made glad with fairest flowers;
May life thus blossom sweetly
In every home of ours.

Jesus, who hast been obedient
To Your parents, to Thee be ever glory,
With the supreme Father
And with the Spirit.   Amen.

The following section contains meditative selections—all poetry, with one exception—that focus on the mystery of the Incarnation.

The Manger He Made
in Celebration of the Lord's Birthday

His highest aim, foremost desire, and greatest intention was
to pay heed to the holy gospel in all things and through all things,
to follow the teaching of our Lord Jesus Christ
and to retrace His footsteps completely
with all vigilance and all zeal,
all the desire of his soul
and all the fervor of his heart.
Francis used to recall with regular meditation the words of Christ
and recollect His deeds with most attentive perception.
Indeed, so thoroughly did the humility of the Incarnation
and the charity of the Passion
occupy his memory
that he scarcely wanted to think of anything else.

We should note, then, as matter worthy of memory and something to be recalled with reverence, what he did, three years prior to his death, at the town of Greccio, on the birthday of our Lord Jesus Christ.

There was a certain man in that area named John who had a good reputation but an even better manner of life. Blessed Francis loved him with special affection, since, despite being a noble in the land and very honored in human society, he had trampled the nobility of the flesh under his feet and pursued instead the nobility of the spirit. As usual, blessed Francis had John summoned to him some fifteen days prior to the birthday of the Lord. "If you desire to celebrate the coming feast of the Lord together at Greccio," he said to him, "hurry before me and carefully make ready the things I tell you. For I wish to enact the memory of that babe who was born in Bethlehem: to see as much as is possible with my own bodily eyes the discomfort of his infant needs, how he lay in a manger, and how, with an ox and an ass standing by, he rested on hay." Once the good and faithful man had heard Francis' words, he ran quickly and prepared in that place all the things that the holy man had requested.

Finally, the day of joy has drawn near,
the time of exultation has come.
From many different places the brethren have been called.
As they could,
the men and women of that land with exultant hearts
prepare candles and torches to light up that night
whose shining star has enlightened every day and year.
Finally, the holy man of God comes
and, finding all things prepared,
he saw them and was glad.
Indeed, the manger is prepared,
the hay is carried in,
and the ox and the ass are led to the spot.
There simplicity is given a place of honor,
poverty is exalted,
humility is commended,
and out of Greccio is made a new Bethlehem.

The night is lit up like day,
delighting both man and beast.
The people arrive, ecstatic at this new mystery of new joy.
The forest amplifies the cries
and the boulders echo back the joyful crowd.
The brothers sing, giving God due praise,

and the whole night abounds with jubilation.
The holy man of God stands before the manger,
filled with heartfelt sighs,
contrite in his piety,
and overcome with wondrous joy.
Over the manger the solemnities of the Mass are celebrated
and the priest enjoys a new consolation.
—The Life of Saint Francis by Thomas of Celano[6]

The Burning Babe

*This is perhaps the best known poem by Saint Robert Southwell, a member
of the Society of Jesus who cared for souls in the London area until his cap-
ture in 1592. He suffered three years' torture and imprisonment and was
executed for his priesthood at Tyburn. He was canonized in 1970.*

As I in hoary winter's night stood shivering in the snow,
Surprised I was with sudden heat which made my heart to
glow;
And lifting up a fearful eye to view what fire was near,
A pretty Babe all burning bright did in the air appear;
Who, scorched with excessive heat, such floods of tears did
shed,
As though his floods should quench his flames which with
his tears were fed.
'Alas!' quoth he, 'but newly born in fiery heats I fry,
Yet none approach to warm their hearts or feel my fire
but I.
My faultless breast the furnace is, the fuel wounding
thorns;
Love is the fire, and sighs the smoke, the ashes shame and
scorns;

The fuel justice layeth on, and mercy blows the coals;
The metal in this furnace wrought are men's defiled souls:
For which, as now on fire I am to work them to their good,
So will I melt into a bath to wash them in my blood.'
With this he vanished out of sight and swiftly shrunk away,
And straight I called unto mind that it was Christmas day.

—Robert Southwell (c. 1561–95)

Psalm for Christmas Day

A well-known preacher in his day, Thomas Pestel was an Anglican divine and sometime chaplain to King Charles I.

Fairest of morning lights appear,
Thou blest and gaudy day,
On which was born our Savior dear;
Arise and come away!

This day prevents His day of doom;
His mercy now is nigh;
The mighty God of Love is come,
The Dayspring from on high.

Behold the great Creator makes
Himself a house of clay,
A robe of Virgin-flesh He takes
Which He will wear for aye.

Hark, hark the wise Eternal Word
Like a weak infant cries:
In form of servant is the Lord,
And God in cradle lies.

This wonder struck the world amazed,
It shook the starry frame;
Squadrons of Spirits stood and gazed,
Then down in troops they came.

Glad Shepherds ran to view this sight;
A quire of Angels sings;
And eastern Sages with delight
Adore this King of kings.

Join then, all hearts that are not stone,
And all our voices prove,
To celebrate this Holy One,
The God of peace and love.

—Thomas Pestel (c. 1584–c. 1659)

From "On the Morning of Christ's Nativity"

Milton, who composed both English and Latin verse, wrote this poem in 1629 while he was at Cambridge.

This is the month, and this the happy morn,
Wherein the Son of heav'n's eternal King,
Of wedded maid and virgin mother born,
Our great redemption from above did bring;
For so the holy sages once did sing,
That he our deadly forfeit should release,
And with His Father work us a perpetual peace.

That glorious form, that light unsufferable,
And that far-beaming blaze of majesty,

Wherewith He wont at heav'n's high council-table
To sit the midst of Trinal Unity,
He laid aside; and here with us to be,
Forsook the courts of everlasting day,
And chose with us a darksome house of mortal clay.

Say, heavenly Muse, shall not thy sacred vein
Afford a present to the infant God?
Hast thou no verse, no hymn, or solemn strain,
To welcome Him to this His new abode;
Now while the heav'n by the sun's team untrod
Hath took no print of the approaching light,
And all the spangled host keep watch in squadrons bright?

See how from far upon the eastern road
The star-led wizards haste with odours sweet:
O run, prevent them with thy humble ode,
And lay it lowly at his blessed feet;
Have thou the honour first, thy Lord to greet,
And join thy voice unto the angel quire,
From out his secret altar touch'd with hallow'd fire.

—John Milton (1608–74)

From "A Cradle Song"

A prolific writer, Watts is considered the creator of the modern hymn, of which he wrote several hundred.

Hush! my dear, lie still and slumber,
Holy angels guard thy bed!
Heavenly blessings without number
Gently falling on thy head.

Sleep, my babe; thy food and raiment,
House and home, thy friends provide;
All without thy care or payment,
All thy wants are well supplied.

How much better thou'rt attended
Than the Son of God could be,
When from heaven He descended,
And became a child like thee!

Soft and easy is thy cradle:
Coarse and hard thy Savior lay:
When His birthplace was a stable,
And His softest bed was hay.

See the kinder shepherds round Him,
Telling wonders from the sky!
Where they sought Him, there they found Him,
With His Virgin Mother by.

See the lovely Babe a-dressing;
Lovely Infant, how He smiled!
When He wept, the Mother's blessing
Soothed and hush'd the holy Child.

Lo, He slumbers in His manger,
Where the hornèd oxen fed;
Peace, my darling, here's no danger;
Here's no ox a-near thy bed!

May'st thou live to know and fear Him,
Trust and love Him all thy days;
Then go dwell for ever near Him,
See His face, and sing His praise!

I could give thee thousand kisses,
Hoping what I most desire;
Not a mother's fondest wishes
Can to greater joys aspire.

—Isaac Watts (1674–1748)

The Lamb

William Blake moved easily between poetry and prose and authored several mystical and metaphysical works. He was also an artist who did many illustrations for the Bible and **Paradise Lost.**

Little Lamb, who made thee?
Dost thou know who made thee?
Gave thee life, and bid thee feed,
By the stream and o'er the mead;
Gave thee clothing of delight,
Softest clothing, woolly, bright;
Gave thee such a tender voice,
Making all the vales rejoice?
Little Lamb, who made thee?
Dost thou know who made thee?
Little Lamb, I'll tell thee,
Little Lamb, I'll tell thee:
He is callèd by thy name,
For He calls Himself a Lamb.
He is meek, and He is mild;
He became a little child.
I a child, and thou a lamb,
We are callèd by His name.
Little Lamb, God bless thee!
Little Lamb, God bless thee!

—William Blake (1757–1827)

In the Bleak Mid-Winter

The author of a number of children's poems, Christina Rossetti was also involved in the Pre-Raphaelite movement, begun by her brother, Dante Gabriel Rossetti, and others.

In the bleak mid-winter
Frosty wind made moan,
Earth stood hard as iron,
Water like a stone;
Snow had fallen, snow on snow,
Snow on snow,
In the bleak mid-winter
Long ago.

Our God, Heaven cannot hold Him,
Nor earth sustain;
Heaven and earth shall flee away
When He comes to reign;
In the bleak mid-winter
A stable-place sufficed
The Lord God Almighty
Jesus Christ.

Enough for Him, whom cherubim
Worship night and day,
A breastful of milk
And a mangerful of hay;
Enough for Him, whom angels
Fall down before,
The ox and ass and camel
Which adore.

Angels and archangels
May have gathered there,
Cherubim and seraphim
Thronged the air;
But only His mother
In her maiden bliss
Worshipped the Belovèd
With a kiss.

What can I give Him,
Poor as I am?
If I were a shepherd
I would bring a lamb,
If I were a Wise Man
I would do my part,
Yet what I can I give Him,
Give my heart.

—Christina Georgina Rossetti (1830–94)

Notes

Introduction

1. Information about this popular and beautiful monthly liturgical publication may be obtained by writing P.O. Box 91, Spencerville, MD 20868, or at Web site www.magnificat.net.
2. See Psalm for Christmas Day, p. 138.
3. If Christmas falls on Sunday, this feast is celebrated on December 30.
4. Ambroise de Lombez, *A Treatise on Interior Peace*, trans. Saint Elizabeth Seton (New York: Alba House, 1996), 80.
5. From a general audience on "Christ's Miracles: Manifestations of Salvific Love," December 9, 1987. See John Paul II, *Wonders and Signs: The Miracles of Jesus* (Boston: St. Paul Books & Media, 1990), 50.
6. Quoted in *The Saint*, vol. 1 of *Francis of Assisi: Early Documents*, ed. Regis J. Armstrong; J. A. Wayne Hellmann; William J. Short, (Hyde Park, N.Y.: New City Press, 1999), 254–56.